Invisible
DIVISION

A Mother's Story of Her Murdered Child, Cheryl Green
(A Victim of a Race Hate Crime)

A Memoir

Charlene Lovett

Professional Publishing House
1425 W. Manchester Ave. Ste B
Los Angeles, California 90047
323-750-3592
Email:www.professionalpublishinghouse@yahoo.com
www.Professionalpublishinghouse.com

Cover design: TWA Solutions
First printing Nov. 2018
978-0-578-42457-6
10987654321

For inquiries contact: charlenelovett@yahoo.com

Dedication

I dedicate this book to everyone who has suffered a tragic, horrific and senseless loss behind hatred because of the color of their skin. I also want to dedicate this book to all the families that have to live a day-to-day reminder that their loved one is no longer here with them in the flesh; however, their spirits live on through the love we carry for them in our hearts. I especially dedicate this book to all the murdered victims of Harbor Gateway whose names were unknown until the death of my daughter, Cheryl Green.

Marquis "Mark" Wilbert, age 11 (1997), Michael Richardson, age 22 (1999), Dino Downs, age 41 (2000), Kent Lopez, age 20 (2000), Robert Hightower, age 19 (2001), Eric Buttler, age 39 (2003). Your names will never be forgotten!

Acknowledgments

I give thanks to The Most High for giving me a forgiving heart. I know with His forgiveness first towards us, we must have forgiveness towards others. I know my immediate forgiveness towards this young man that murdered my daughter was the cause of all the positive results that came.

I thank God for His strength, courage and His inspiration in writing this book. All Praises, Honor and Glory is due to Him the Creator, Who is the Head of my life. HalleluYah!

I also want to thank Troy Harris who kept me motivated, being a cheerleader and all the time, keeping me in her prayers while writing this book. She helped by keeping me focused and staying the course. My cousin and best friend, I love you. Thank you so much!

To Milton Mc Daniel, III, thank you for taking the time to pre-read and pre-edit each chapter as I was writing this book. Your dedication was immeasurable and you did it with pleasure! I thank you with all my heart!

To Alex Alonso, I appreciate your support towards helping me get this book published. By you referring me to Dr. Rosie Milligan, it happened. I am deeply grateful!

Dr. Rosie Milligan, you have beauty of grace, degrees of knowledge and distinguished wisdom. You are a light to me and I'm sure to many others. Your support and mentorship fills up the atmosphere with your compassion! I thank you sincerely from the depths of my heart.

TO ALL I HAVE ACKNOWLEDGED, I LOVE YOU ALL...
LOVETT

My Seasonal Introduction

The Move In

In August, during the summer of 2000, my four children and I were excited as we approached our new three-bedroom apartment, ready for a new beginning. I thought to myself, "Finally," until I could afford to buy a home. I found a place where I didn't hear much about gang violence on the news every day. I found a place where my children and I would be safe, relative to the other neighborhoods we'd lived, which were plagued with gangs and all the negative activities that comes along with a gang-life style. We were happy we were settling in—not knowing, "WE MOVED OUT OF THE FRYING PAN INTO THE FIRE" (Oh, my Goodness!).

Within the next few days, my neighbors gave me "warnings" about the neighborhood. Do not go pass 206th Street and absolutely never go to the Del Amo Market on 204th Street. "There's a Hispanic gang over there that hates black people, and if you are caught in 'their' territory, you could be killed!"

My mouth opened wide; I was in shock, listening to what they were telling me. One neighbor shared an incident that happened a year prior to me moving in. It was about the people who lived one apartment building up from me. In 1999, the former resident, named Elizabeth, went grocery shopping with her boyfriend, Michael, and after returning home, they began unloading their groceries into their apartment. One of the Hispanic gang members walked from the other side of the street with a shotgun, shooting. Michael was shot in the back and died from the injury. My first thought was it had to be more to the story. It was hard to believe that this gang killed him just because he was Black. I was thinking maybe it was gang-on-gang violence. Then a week later, I got an unexpected knock on my front door.

The Knock

There was a knock at my door, so I asked, "Who is it?" From the answer I received, I became nervous. It was the homicide investigators looking for the previous tenants. Supposedly, the previous tenants witnessed the shooting of Michael, who was killed a year earlier. They asked my name and said, "Are you the person who saw the shooting that happened to the neighbor a year ago?"

I responded, "No. I just moved in about a week ago."

Then they asked, "You know where the previous tenants moved to?"

Feeling as if they did believe that I was the person who actually witnessed the murder, I responded again, "No, I don't know."

They gave me their Los Angeles Police Detective cards and said give it to the previous tenants, if I happen to see or hear from them.

After that encounter with the homicide detectives, I started believing what the neighbors had told me and advised my children of all the restrictions of the neighborhood. I told them never to go past 206th Street; this is where the "invisible line" exists. This information kept me on high alert, at all times!

In the year 2000, my son, David, was twelve, my oldest daughter, Vanessa, was eleven, Allena, my middle daughter was nine, and my baby-girl, Cheryl, was seven. In the beginning, they enjoyed staying in, entertaining one another, but after seeing all the neighborhood kids outside, they wanted to go out to meet them, and they did.

Summer was ending. It was time to enroll the kids into school. It was also time to go over the neighborhood restrictions again. They enjoyed school and riding on the city bus as it was the first time they had to use public transportation to get back and forth from school. They knew to only get on and off the city bus on 208th Street and Western Ave., where it was supposed to be safe. We were thriving, the kids were in school and I worked. We knew our restrictions and boundaries, our going out and our coming in was an all-time routine. Whenever family or friends came to visit, I would tell them what streets to drive down, keeping them away from 204th Street. I explained the potential danger of being on that street as a Black person. However, as careful as you thought you were, you could never be careful enough!

It was springtime, April 2001. There were lots of neighbors outside. There were police cars everywhere with a helicopter circling over 206th and 207th Street. I also noticed paramedics were on the scene. Something tragic had happened! I walked to the corner of my street to get a closer look and a few feet from me a Black man lay in the street—dead. Later that evening, the story was out.

The man's name was Eric Buttler. He and his children were visiting family that lived on Harvard Blvd, between 206th and 207th Street. His teenaged daughter walked to the Del Amo Market on 204th Street (unaware of the danger) and started receiving verbal assaults by the Hispanic gang members at the market. She called Eric, her father, on her cell phone, told him to pick her up from the market and he did. The gang members followed them back to their location, which was on Harvard Blvd, close to 207th Street. They began shooting at Eric and his children.

At this point, I realized that this Hispanic gang hated Black people. The neighborhood was on high alert, and we were definitely afraid and in fear living in our Los Angeles neighborhood. They would come out to target Blacks during school breaks, summers and holidays. It was the perfect opportunity for them to commit their violent, hateful, and horrific crimes.

That summer, Mark, a Black teenager, was shot; thank YAH he did not die. However, Black people continued to be their target with racial slurs spray painted on the walls of apartment buildings, stop signs and street curbs. It would say, "Fuck Niggas."

My family and I never discriminated, felt hatred, or disliked someone because of their skin color, culture, or religion. As a Black family, we were taught to love and respect everyone. All people from all places!

Season One

Life Altered

In December 2006, I began apartment searching. I had a feeling of urgency and desperation to get my family out of this neighborhood, the Harbor Gateway area, not knowing the tragedy we were about to face. The morning of December 15th, I got out of bed to see my youngest daughter off to school, but there was a sadness in my spirit. I prayed to YAHWEH, asking, "Why I am feeling this way?"

Then the voice of the Most High told me there will be a shooting today. This is the first time feeling very uncomfortable in my spirit so I questioned my 14-year-old daughter. Although knowing the answers such as, "What bus stop are you going to and who with?" After some reassurance that she was staying within the boundaries, I allowed her to leave for school. I was under the weather that particular day and decided to stay in to rest. Because it was the last day of school before Winter break, Cheryl had come home early.

I called out to her, "Cheryl," but she didn't respond.

I called her name again and finally she answered, "Yes, Mommy."

"Don't go anywhere," I told her.

I stayed awake, lying in the bed, then twenty minutes later, someone was frantically knocking and kicking on my front door. I quickly opened it and standing there was Cheryl's best friend, Hanifa, who was 17 years old at that time. sobbing uncontrollably.

"Cheryl was shot," she said between her loud cries.

The words coming out of her mouth sounded foreign to me, as if she was talking another language.

She continued saying, "Cheryl was shot."

After a few more seconds, it became clearer to me what she said. Staying as calm as I could, I put my clothes and shoes on, combed my hair (a little) and left for the hospital, which was only four blocks away from where we lived. However, it was the longest two-minute ride I ever had.

I prayed in the car, asking, "YAH, where she was shot?"

"He said three people were shot, the hand, stomach, and the side of the body."

I arrived at the emergency entrance and quickly got out of the car, walking fast into the hospital.

When I walked to the receptionist I said, "My daughter was shot and brought to this hospital." She looked as if she didn't know what to say.

"I said my name is Charlene Lovett, and my daughter Cheryl was shot and brought to this hospital."

My oldest daughter, Vanessa, was standing with me when she said, "Wait for the Chaplain." At this point, I was just going through the motions with no feelings. While walking to the Chapel, I thought to myself, she said go wait in the "Chapel." This is not good, then I thought, *Maybe she's in surgery;, she'll be fine!* As we walked towards

12

the Chapel, we passed a lot of Black people who were there from our neighborhood.

After going inside, waiting for the Chaplain, Vanessa and I didn't know what to say to each other. We didn't know what to think, nor how to feel. We just stood there waiting for someone to come in and tell us what was going on. There were people knocking on the door, but I only allowed family and close friends to enter. While I waited for someone to come and talk with me, my son, my ex-husband, and his father walked in. We all had looks of uncertainty in our eyes.

The doctor came in with a look of sympathy, "I'm sorry," he said. "She didn't make it."

I looked him in his eyes, grabbed his hand, and nodded my head. "Okay." I was numb.

"I'm sorry," he said and walked out.

I had to stay strong for my son and daughter because as soon as they heard the doctor say she didn't make it, they all started sobbing uncontrollably. My middle daughter, Allena, and her little cousin, LaToya, walked in. When they saw everyone crying, they began crying, too, knowing Cheryl was no longer with us. Allena punched the wall in anger while my cousin, LaToya, was praying, "God, bring my little cousin back. Please, God! Bring my little cousin back!"

Then my mother walked in. She knew immediately Cheryl had died. She cried, holding me tight.

Cheryl's father, Lenwood, had passed away three years earlier from a brain hemorrhage. They were very close. Lenwood and I divorced in 1995, but after our divorce, we agreed on joint custody. She spent a lot of time with him. She was Daddy's little girl and he loved her, and she loved him. The next step was to call his family and tell them.

Since there was a police station next door from the Chaplain's office, I went to use their phone and noticed more Black people from my neighborhood were there. They were sad, sobbing and in disbelief.

I walked into the police station and asked the lady at the front desk, "May I use the phone?"

"Yes," she replied.

I dialed Wanda's cell number, Cheryl's aunt, and she answered, "Hello." Trying to get the words out of my mouth, I said, "Wanda... Cheryl was killed today."

She yelled, "WHAT?"

I said it again, "Wanda, they killed Cheryl. They killed my baby!"

Then it hit me. I started sobbing, I was trying to tell her, but ran to the back of the police station. I began to see images of myself in the delivery room giving birth to Cheryl, I held my stomach because I could feel the labor pains all over again and I sat in there sobbing.

After returning back to the phone, I said, "Wanda, they killed Chery; they killed my baby!"

I dropped the phone, sitting there weeping and motionless.

The lady from the front desk ran out of the police station to get someone, returning with my mom who rocked and held me for a while until I was coherent again. My mom left to find a doctor to medicate me, but after sitting there a while I became calm.

When I walked out of the police station, it seemed as if YAH said, "Okay, everyone take your places, action!" People I did not know, one by one, came to me with information.

A lady named Wanda gave me her business card and said, "I'll do your obituaries free." Then a man named Herald from grievance and family support gave me his card; consequently, he was the one who provided the funeral service for Cheryl. Another man from Harbor City who represented "The Victim of Crimes," founded by the government, which provides financial support to victims who have suffered or died from acts of violence.

The Most High had given me all the information I needed to go forth with making funeral arrangements before leaving the hospital.

When I returned to the Chaplain, my grandmother, aunties, cousins, in-laws, and close friends were there. We formed a circle, took one another by the hand and prayed for His unmeasurable peace and understanding that not my will, but His will be done. When I left the Chaplain, more people from the community was there. The Most High had given me strength and I was able to comfort them and let them know it will be all right. YAH is so amazing!

I asked the doctor could I see my baby, but the detectives told me that her body was evidence. If any evidence was found on her body, they didn't want it disturbed. I understood. I definitely didn't want to hinder their investigation and prevent them from catching my daughter's killer.

Returning Home

When we pulled up to my apartment building, many of the neighbors were standing outside crying and some were very angry. I somewhat greeted them as I went inside my apartment.

I heard a knock on my door and it was my ex-husband.

He was outraged saying that he was going to 204th Street for revenge.

I grabbed him saying, "No, you're not. My daughter's death will not be in vain.

We're going to handle it the way The Most High wants us to."

He understood that I was serious, and he calmed down before he left.

There was another knock at the door.

It was a neighbor saying, "I'm going on 204th to shoot the street up."

I expressed to him the same feelings I told my ex-husband, "It will be handled with peace."

Although it took a while to settle him down, he, too, was calmed before leaving.

I went into Cheryl's bedroom and looked around. Once again, I started crying. A year prior, Cheryl and I had painted her walls pink. Her comforter on her bed was also pink. She was in love with the R&B group B2K and had plenty of their posters on her bedroom walls, along with other magazine clippings. She loved the television cartoon SpongeBob and had a SpongeBob-stuffed character laid with her pillows. Cheryl's pants, shirts, jackets and sweaters were hung neatly in her closet, but her shoes were a different story. They were in a pile inside the closet. I walked inside her closet and started smelling her clothes so that I could get a smell of her scent and cried. "I can't believe you would never be coming home again," I said.

I went to my bathroom and wept, continuously.

A few months earlier, I had bought Cheryl a Bible and I would see her reading it.

One day I asked her, "Do you believe that YahShuha died on the cross for us?"

She said, "Yes."

I then asked, "Do you accept YahShuha as your personal Savior?"

She said, "Yes,"

I told her, "You are saved." (John 3:16, "For YAH so loved the world that He gave His only begotten Son, that whoever believes in Him should not perish, but have everlasting life.") I knew she was in the bosom of The Most High, yet I deeply mourned her. I thought about how I would no longer look into her slanted brown eyes, feel the touch of her soft skin, nor would I hear the sound of her bubbly voice.

Making Phone Calls

My older sister lives in Jacksonville, North Carolina, but was vacationing in Miami at the time of Cheryl's death. I dialed her cell phone with tears running down my face. She answered saying, "Hello, little sis."

I said, "Sis… Cheryl was killed today—my baby—she's gone. Someone killed her."

She dropped the phone screaming, "No…no…!"

My brother-in-law, Maurice, who, at the time was serving in the Marines Corp., got on the phone. "What's going on?" he asked.

When I told him that Cheryl was murdered, holding in his emotions, he said with a steely voice, "I will get her on the next plane leaving for Los Angeles."

The next phone call I had to make would be even tougher than the first one. I spoke to my cousin, Rachel, about a very disturbing vision I had in my sleep about six to seven months prior. In the dream my middle daughter was lying in a hospital bed with tubes in her and an oxygen mask on her face. She had gotten shot on the side of her body.

In the dream, I began praying, praying so hard that she would be all right. I jumped up out of my sleep, my heart beating rapidly. I remembered Rachel telling me sometimes it's not the person in the dream. She also advised me to keep Cheryl close to me. (In the book of Joel 2:28, "And it shall come to pass afterward that I will pour out My Spirit on all flesh; your sons and your daughters will prophesy.")

When Rachel answered her phone, I was crying so hard, she said. "Stop crying. I can't understand what you're saying." But I was uncontrollable. I continued crying. "Stop crying, Charlene," she said. "I can't hear you."

Finally, I stopped long enough to tell her, then I heard the phone drop. After getting back on the phone, she said, "I'm on my way."

I returned back into my bedroom and thought about when I was pregnant with Cheryl. I just couldn't understand why, why my baby— why her? However, as time went on, I began to understand.

I heard a knock at the door. I got up and answered the door. It was Rachel and her sister, Regina, so I let them in. Soon people from the neighborhood came and I welcomed them in, too. We held each other's hand and prayed, asking The Most High for the capture of the person, or persons, who killed Cheryl. We also we prayed for protection of all Blacks in the neighborhood. After prayer, Regina asked, "Does anyone want to accept YahuShua into their life as their personal Savior?"

Yes! Five people were saved that night. (Praise YAH).

Later that night, I was given a sleeping pill to help me sleep. I went to my bedroom and wept. As I laid in bed, I thought back to the time of giving birth to Cheryl. I saw myself lying in hospital bed in labor, knowing Cheryl was ready to come.

I remember telling the nurse I have to push, but she said, "No, don't push."

I told her again, "I need to push!"

When she looked between my legs and saw Cheryl's head, she ran out the hospital room, yelling for the doctor. Two minutes later, Cheryl was born and placed into my arms.

I prayed, "Abba YAH, give me strength." I repeated, "Father, I need Your strength!"

Season Two

T he sleeping pill that was given to me the night before did the job because I had an uninterrupted sleep, but when I woke up that morning, it hit me all over again! I got down on my knees. "YAH, continue to give me strength, in Jesus's (YahuShua's) name I pray, HalleluYah."

I didn't have an appetite that morning, I went into the living room with my children, and we hugged each other, staying strong for one another.

Making the Arrangements

Friday morning, approximately 9:00 a.m., I started making phone calls a mother never thought, or even fathomed to think about making; however, with YAH'S strength I proceeded to make them. The first phone call I made was to the hospital to see if the coroner had picked up Cheryl's body. The answer was no; I was asked to call back Monday. Then I called "Victims of Crime" and set an appointment to meet Monday evening. Finally, I called the mortuary and spoke with Herald, the director. We arranged a meeting for the following day.

Family, friends and neighbors visited my children and me throughout the day, bringing food, sympathy cards and donations. The day was surrounded with love and support.

Later that evening, Vanessa and my cousin, Latoya, called Fox 11, the local news station. They told them about Cheryl's death and informed me that a news reporter would like to come interview me. Also, they would be covering the candle-light vigil we were having for Cheryl on the news. Moments before the vigil, someone knocked on the door.

It was the news reporter asking could she interview me. I replied, "Yes," and welcomed Jane Yamamoto in.

We sat down at my dining room table, and then she asked, "What happened?"

"I really don't know," I said. "All I can tell you is from the time Cheryl came home from school, until I got the knock on my door."

Then she asked, "What was the last thing you said to your daughter?"

I responded, "Don't go anywhere." She thanked me and proceeded in covering the vigil where Cheryl was killed.

When we walked outside, there were people standing in line on both sides of the sidewalk with their candles lit. We joined in and started walking to where Cheryl was killed. When we arrived at the corner of 207th and Harvard, more people were there with their candles lit. There I stood, approximately eight feet from 20607 S. Harvard, close to the driveway where my daughter was murdered. Crying and afraid of what I was about to see, I slowly walked to the driveway. I stared at the ground where she died; her blood was still there. Everyone sobbed in sorrow.

I looked down at the two little girls Cheryl used to babysit. Their eyes were filled with tears when they asked me, "Where is Cheryl?"

Their mother responded, "In Heaven."

My heart was sympathetic to their young minds, knowing they didn't understand that they would never see Cheryl again. Rachel began praying, "YAH, let there be peace and harmony in this community."

We hugged each other and encouraged one another, gaining strength. The horrendous acts of racism we had suffered in the neighborhood, we knew must come to an end. The vigil lasted a little over an hour with approximately 150 concerned neighbors, family, friends and people who felt the compassion to come out and give support.

That night we became united, ready to take a stand!

After returning home, I turned on the television to watch the news. It was surreal to see my family as a top story—a news tragedy.

December 17, 2006, I went to the hospital to see how the other teens that were injured from the shooting were doing. I spoke with their family members and was told they were doing well. Nicole had to have surgery on her right hand. Donald, who was shot in the stomach, where the bullet went in and out, was okay. Isadream, the other victim, had a bullet which skinned the side of her head. She was released from the hospital the same day of the shooting. I was also told that the detectives visited with them and they were able to give descriptions of the shooter. I hugged them and left.

There were lots of concerned people coming by to give us support and I appreciated it very much, but, I asked my mom to place a "Do not disturb sign" on the door.

I wanted and needed some alone time with my children, when I returned home. I was told from my mom and cousin that when I was at the hospital, two men disregarded the sign and knocked on the door. Accordingly, to the men they said the sign didn't apply to them; consequently, they were correct.

It was community activist, Najee Ali, who have supported Blacks and other minorities in their time of unjust treatment, such as unlawful actions and racial discrimination. Also, I met Melvin Snells, who stands against injustices of the people as well. After both of them seeing me on the news, they were ready to take action and help end the racial violence that plagued that neighborhood. Ali and Snells spoke with my mom and cousin for a while, then donated a hundred dollars to my family and left their business cards.

After getting that information, I called Najee, but, he didn't answer. However, calling Melvin was a success. We discussed actions that needed to happen, such as protesting, marches and media coverage to unveil the racial killings that secretly had been occurring in the community. While talking with him on the phone, I could feel the presence of The Most High, He was speaking through Melvin. Afterwards, we ended the phone call with prayer.

Season Three

The funeral director was arriving soon, and I knew I needed super-natural strength to endure the meeting, so I went to my bedroom for prayer. I greeted him at the door, welcoming him in. He spoke softly as he introduced his self and giving me his condolence. We sat down at the dining room table. He gave me a photo album of different styles of caskets. I took my time, carefully considering every detail of the casket that I would be choosing to lay my baby-girl in, to rest. Cheryl's favorite color was pink, so I chose the pink pearl-rose casket. It had gold angels on the corners and on each side of the casket. The inside was lined with pink satin. I also wanted fourteen doves released to represent the years we had with her, at the end of service. Cheryl was to be buried with her father at the Veterans cemetery. Choosing to bury her at the Veterans Cemetery was the best choice. Ergo, she became a veteran for the lives she saved. Before the meeting ended, the director advised me to select the clothes I wanted her dressed in. He would have someone retrieve them within a few days. Also I was to call him with the date of service.

The Bible says in Isaiah 40:29 that YAH gives power to the faint and weary and to him who has no might, YAH increases strength (causing it to multiply and making it to abound). He truly did! (Thank You, YAHWEH, for Your Strength!)

Monday morning, I awoke in prayer, knowing the day would be challenging. I called the hospital to see if they picked up Cheryl's body and the answer was "yes," however, I still could not see her or arrange for the mortuary to pick her up. I spoke with the lady who offered to do the obituaries. She told me to write down what I wanted it to say and she would organize it.

I left for my meeting with the Victims of Crime in San Pedro. When I walked in Mrs. Irvine's office, she was immediately supportive and compassionate as she gave me the application to fill out. I was quickly approved for the full funeral, burial cost, relocation expenses, grievance counseling for my children and myself. I was thankful!

When I walked into my apartment, there was a local news journalist named Larry Altman, interviewing my mother and children.

I sat on the arm rest of my sofa when he said, "Tell me about your youngest daughter."

I burst out in tears and could not speak. It was strange because as hard as I was crying, I started laughing just as hard. A vision of Cheryl came to me while I was crying about a baby shower we attended a week before she was killed. My daughters and I attended a friend's baby shower. Male exotic dancers came into the room and started dancing. Unfortunately, I didn't know they were going to be there, so I grabbed Cheryl and sat her next to me. When I went to the restroom and returned, Cheryl was not sitting where I left her. I looked around and saw that she moved to get a closer look, I said, "Cheryl!" She turned around and looked at me with her big beautiful smile, and then we both started laughing.

Once again, neighbors, family and friends came with their condolences, giving sympathy cards, food and more donations. However, some Blacks from nearby cities came with violence in mind, asking me did I want retaliation.

I told them "No, that's not the way we're going to handle it." I know YAHWEH is on my side. Whatever the Devil meant for bad, YAHWEH will turn it around for good, for His glory! Sharing the day with my family and childhood friends was great. Their love and support were much needed and deeply appreciated. I shared the rest of the evening peacefully with my children.

The next morning, the local newspaper was out with the headline, "Girl, 14, May Be the Latest Victim of a Hate Crime."

According to Robert Casillas from the *"Daily Breeze,"* a Los Angeles police Detective, David Cortez, said, "They are investigating it as a hate crime."

Another Detective, Mike Falvo, stated, "It's another senseless act of violence; it's pretty disgusting."

In the newspaper, there was a story of an eleven-year-old black boy, who was killed by a Hispanic gang member in 1997, a couple of blocks from where Cheryl died.

According to the Black neighborhood kids and my son, the local police would see them around the neighborhood and would suggest they go home to be safe. Ironically, we went along with the program, as if it was normal. No one who knew about the past killings brought any attention to the fact that Blacks were being targeted for "Ethnic cleansing." Because of the news article, it started the beginning of a full-blown investigation into the history of the neighborhood. Until then no one knew there was such a big problem—RACISM!

Cheryl's best friend, Hanifa, came to my apartment to tell me about her last interactions with Cheryl, moments before she died. Cheryl went to Hanifa's apartment, wanting her to come outside, but she was in bed. Cheryl told her, "Get up, sleepy head." Since she didn't get out of bed, Cheryl told her, "I'm going around the corner. I'll be back."

A few hours later, one of the victims who was not injured, came to my apartment to tell Allena and myself what she saw in the driveway where Cheryl was killed. According to Sadae, Cheryl was coming from 206th Street when she saw them standing in their driveway. She stopped to talk with them. Sadae said Cheryl was there about two minutes when a male Hispanic walked up, pointed his gun towards her six-year-old brother and her nineteen-year-old cousin, Buckner, then squeezed the trigger twice, but the gun was jammed. He then pointed the gun towards Cheryl and the others, then started shooting. She said Cheryl stood there frozen, unable to move, looking at him while urinating on herself. I can't begin to imagine what she was thinking as a gun was being pointed in her direction. "I'm about to die," could have been her last thought. Sadae continued telling me that as he was shooting, some jumped over a fence and others ran. Then the shooter ran. She saw everything that happened as she hid under a car.

After they knew it was safe, everyone returned to the driveway and saw Cheryl lying on the ground shot in the side with blood coming out of her mouth. As she was telling me what happened, I could picture the images in my mind. In the midst of her telling me what happened, I wanted to scream, "Shut up!" but I needed to know. She continued telling us how Buck tried to put Cheryl in the car, but she was too heavy and dropped her. I'm thinking, "He dropped her!" She said Cheryl was already gone; that's why she was hard to lift.

Finally, they all helped and got her in the car, then took her to the hospital. I could not believe I just heard how my baby died. It was horrible. I sat there, unable to move for a while. Then I went into my bedroom and cried myself to sleep.

In the morning, I called the coroner's office again, but they still had not released her body. I became irritated. It had been five days now and I still hadn't been able to see her. I went into prayer, "ABBA, keep her body preserved." I had faith He would and felt relieved.

I left to pick out flower arrangements for the funeral. I walked inside and asked the florist, "May I see a book of floral arrangements?"

"Oh, yes. Is this for a wedding?" she asked.

I started sobbing. "No, it's for my daughter's funeral."

After saying that, she became aware of who I was. She was very apologetic and then told me that her daughter worked at the hospital where Cheryl was brought in as a patient. She also told me that her daughter was one of the nurses who tried to help resuscitate her. I was in awe of what she told me and began to realize this was bigger than me. YAH's preordained will was being revealed. She gave me her condolences and was very helpful as I picked out the pink and white flower arrangements.

When I returned home, I went to my bedroom for prayer. "ABBA, let the detectives catch the murderer who killed my daughter."

I heard the voice of YAH like never before when He said, "Surely they will catch him; he will die."

I quickly jumped up because I've never heard YAH's voice so powerful—so direct like that before. However, at that moment, my faith was stronger! Then I heard a knock on the door.

I was greeted by the Los Angeles Police Detectives Falvo and Webber. They showed empathy while giving me their condolences. We sat at the dining room table as they told me about the leads they had on the case and about the raids they performed on 204th Street and near-by cities. Also, they made several arrests. After the information they gave me, I looked Detective Falvo in his eyes and with super-natural faith said, "You will catch him."

He looked back at me with a question in his eyes. "You know something we don't know?" Before leaving they gave me their cards. "Give us a call if you have any questions or need anything."

I thought about how to dress Cheryl for her "Home-Going Celebration." Then the Holy Spirit counseled me, whoever accepts Yahushua (Jesus) as their Savior becomes His Bride. (Ephesians 5:25 says husbands, love your wives as Yahushua loved the church and gave Himself up for her).

I took my daughters and their friend Shelly to "David's Bridals," to select a wedding dress for Cheryl. While looking at dresses I kept thinking, I'm here to buy a wedding dress for Cheryl to be buried in. Sobbing uncontrollably, I was unable to stand. A sales assistant came over to inquire about the situation. Vanessa, my oldest daughter, told her about the loss of their sister. The sales assistant was speechless at first, but then she showed empathy and had compassion while conversing with us. She left, but returned with a chair for me to sit in. She selected several different styles of gowns for me to choose from.

Finally, I chose a beautiful white-beaded gown with a big bow on the lower back. I asked the sales assistant to have the bow removed and given to me. My daughters picked out a tiara with small white pearls around it, dropped pearl earrings, a beautiful necklace with a pearl-drop in front, a pair of white-satin gloves, and a pair of pearl-white ballerina slippers. Since Shelly was the same height and size as Cheryl, I asked Shelly to try the dress on for measurements.

After the measurements were taken, the sales assistant said, "The gown will be ready the following day, and I will personally deliver the dress to you."

After giving her the information needed for delivery, I thanked her for her kindness.

When I returned home, I called Najee Ali. He shared some knowledge with me regarding the history of this gang and their violence towards Blacks.

Then he asked, "Are you willing to take a stand against this gang and their hatred towards Blacks in this community?"

"Yes, I'm willing—I'm ready!"

So, we agreed to meet the following day.

I sat down to write Cheryl's obituary. I asked my children if they wanted to write something to their sister. They all said, "Yes!" My cousin, Cheryl's best friend, and Shelly wrote poems, too. The front of the obituary would have a picture of Cheryl, also throughout it, pictures of her dad, siblings and me graced the obituary. Her newborn footprints would be copied on a page with a poem saying, "If I knew it would be the last time that I saw you walk out the door, I would give you a hug, a kiss and call you back for one more."

I also included a list of things Cheryl liked, such as taking pictures, reading, writing poems, listening to music, spending time with her family, and enjoying home cooked food. She was humble with a bubbly personality, a smile that was super-contagious and she loved her family deeply. Her spirit was meek, and she had wisdom—way beyond her years. When it was time for me to write who she left behind, I got very emotional! My grandmother, at eighty-two, who outlived her fourteen siblings and a host of friends, now had outlived her fourteen-year-old great-granddaughter who was now included on that list. It was dreadful to write. Writing the obituary was a painful task to complete. Cheryl's great-grandmother has since passed in 2009 at the age of 85.

In completing the obituary, I gave thanks to everyone for their love, support and prayers.

That day, December 22th, my sister was arriving, and I decided to pick her up from the airport so I could have some alone time with her before bringing her to the family, but in the meantime, there were phone calls I needed to make. I called the coroner's office again and this time the answer was "Yes, she's been released."

Now I was able to set a date for the funeral services. Taking in consideration it was close to Christmas, I chose not to have a viewing for her. I wanted everyone to enjoy Christmas as best as they could. So, I chose to have the funeral on December 27th. I called the director of the mortuary and he confirmed the date.

I met with Najee and Melvin to discuss what would take place for tomorrow and, "Yes," I was ready! Najee told me about the many phone calls he'd made and how Los Angeles Councilwoman Janice Hahn would be here for our news conference the following day.

I received a phone call from the bridal shop from the sales assistant, letting me know she would deliver the dress later this evening, but for now, it was time to leave for the LAX airport. On my way to the airport, I could already see the images of the sorrow, hurt, pain, compassion, but more than all the disbelief my sister probably was feeling. I was preparing myself to tell her all that had taken place since Cheryl's death, plus the upcoming press conference that we, and the media was having the following morning. I felt so many mixed emotions at one time.

When I saw my sister coming down the escalator, I began to cry. I walked up, grabbed her and told her I was so thankful she was here. I told her about activists, Najee and Melvin, also told her about the news conference we were having in the morning.

Upon returning home, the family was happy to see her. Rachel said, "Good you're here. Now I can go home and get some things." She hadn't left my side since the "Day."

Later that evening, Cheryl's dress was delivered from the bridal shop with blessings from the sales assistant.

The morning of the press conference, I went into prayer. "Heavenly Father, continue to give me strength and peace that surpasses all understanding in Yahushua's Name, Amen." Indeed, He did!

Najee and Melvin arrived. "Are you ready?" they asked.

"Yes," I said.

Then my family gathered together and walked to the driveway where Cheryl was killed. The closer we got, the slower I walked. I stopped, took a deep breath and started to cry, but I continued to walk to the driveway. I looked at the shrine that was made for her. Then I looked directly at the place where she died. Her blood was still there. We all sobbed terribly.

Councilwoman Janice Hahn, who was over the district at that time, arrived. Hahn is also the daughter of the former Los Angeles County Supervisor Kenneth Hahn, Sr.

It is important to me to give a little history of Hahn Sr. because Councilwoman Hahn has modeled in her father's footsteps. He allowed a major baseball team to enter into Los Angeles, put freeway call boxes on the freeway, and the idea of paramedics to assist people in emergency. He was very supportive towards civil rights. In 1961, Hahn was the only politician to welcome Dr. Martin Luther Jr. to Los Angeles. After Dr. King was assassinated, he fought to have a hospital named after Dr. King. Hahn stayed in Los Angeles political office for forty-five years.

Janice Hahn walked up to me, gave me her condolences, and the news conference began. When I spoke, I asked that no one try to avenge her death. I also asked for the gun man to surrender, to turn his self in. We called for peace! Hoping to end the racial division in the community that Cheryl's death would spawn a peace-movement and as you continue to read you will see that's exactly what happened.

As we stood there, I felt peace in the community. I told them, "I see peace in Harbor-Gateway, peace from 190th St. to Torrance Boulevard. Cheryl's death was a sacrifice to bring peace to this community."

Councilwoman Hahn, sobbing while hugging me, said, "I promise to you this will not happen again. I will put every resource in this community."

Najee stated, "It is outrageous that African American children are fearful, they cannot walk two blocks over from this invisible dividing line. This is not apartheid, this is not South Africa."

The news conference was covered in the newspaper the following morning.

The police and the residents scheduled a town hall meeting. Najee, Melvin and my family planned a peace march for December 30th. I was on fire! I had power from The Most High and my spirit was willing!

There were many interviews from news reporters, radio personalities and magazine journalists. Everything was moving quickly, and prayer was the only way to be effective!

The following day, late in the evening, my 15-year-old daughter, Allena, came into my bedroom to talk with me. She had something very important to tell me. Sitting on my bed she said, "I'm pregnant."

My mouth went wide open. Wow, I didn't expect to hear that coming from her. I was conflicted, not knowing how to respond, at first.

Then I asked, "What are you going to do?"

Her reply was, "I'm going to have this baby."

I said, "Okay, we will talk more about this soon."

Later that evening I thought about our conversation and reasoned, Cheryl's life was taken, now another life has been given. *I will be a grandmother*! I was delighted!

December 25, 2006, in the morning I was awakened to twenty plus family members in my apartment with catered breakfast. I was so surprised and thankful! It was Christmas and my family showed the meaning of what Christmas was, "Giving!" They gave to me what money could never buy—"Love!"

We ate together, talked with each other, took pictures and made memories that will last forever. In the midst of the pain in our hearts, love prevailed.

The following day I received a phone call from, LAPD detective, Falvo. He told me that the man who was the look-out for the shooter had been arrested. A twenty-year-old Hispanic male named Ernesto Alcarez was charged with premeditated murder and six counts of attempted murder, all hate-crimes. I was thankful, very grateful and relived! I knew it wouldn't be long for the shooter to be identified and captured.

There were some family members over to help me prepare for the funeral. We chose to wear pink in our clothing to represent Cheryl. My sister-in-law, Jeanie, was helpful with buying a grey, pink-pinstripe pants suit and a pink shirt for me to wear. I had many different emotions, feelings and thoughts about the funeral. The time was drawing near. It would be the first time seeing my baby again; however, it would also be the last.

Late that evening, everyone was home, but somber and very quiet. No one talked about the day we were about to face. It was as if we were communicating with each other without saying a word. I think we were afraid to express how we were feeling, but we were on the same accord. We said our goodnights and went to bed.

Season Four

Peacefully Going Home

I awoke, bent down on my knees and prayed, "ABBA, I need You! Carry me through this day in Jesus's (Yahushua's) name, Amen." I stayed in that position for a while before rising. I received several phone calls that morning from people making sure of the correct time and directions of where the service was being held. Everyone in the house was preparing themselves for the funeral.

When Cheryl's family from her dad's side arrived, I became emotional because Cheryl's first cousin resembled her so much. When she walked in, I stared at her, then hugged her tightly. The funeral was being held at Faithful Central Bible Church, 400 W. Florence Ave., in Inglewood. I requested that the limo get us to the church early. I wanted and needed time alone with Cheryl.

Riding in the limo, it seemed like it took forever getting us to the church. It felt like the same ride, like the ride to the hospital the day Cheryl was killed. I couldn't wait for the limo driver to formally open the door like they normally do. I let myself out. I had waited long enough to see my baby. I got out and quickly walked into the church. I continued walking fast until I approached her casket. I looked up and whispered, "YAH, give me strength," I took a deep breath and then looked down. My baby was laid out beautifully, and peacefulness filled the atmosphere.

My thought was, "Cheryl, get up!" In that same thought, I knew she wouldn't. She was in heaven with our Creator, with her father and family. We stayed with her as long as we could before the service started. I told her how much I loved her, how I will miss her and I will carry the memories of her forever in my heart.

The *Los Angeles Times* photographer and news reporter was setting up their equipment to share the funeral service with the world. I wanted the world to see—to know about the racial hatred that plagued our neighborhood. The pain it caused my family and the community, but also, I wanted people who were willing to come and help heal the community.

Pastor Allen asked me would we like to be seated when the guests arrived, or would we proceed in after the guests arrived. I chose to be seated before they arrived. I believe the family of the deceased sets the tone of the funeral. When the family enters in after the guests have been seated, they look at each person. They see the hurt, the pain in their faces and fall apart. I did not want that. I wanted the "Peace" that surpasses all understanding surrounding everyone—and it did. YAH's presence and His peace filled the building!

During the service, family members and friends gave beautiful testimonies of Cheryl. Councilwoman Hahn said empathically, "I'm sorry and I hope Cheryl's death will mend the neighborhood."

Pastor Allen gave an amazing eulogy! My cousin, Cheryl, who Cheryl was named after, asked, "Who wants to know Jesus (Yahushua) Stand up."

I looked behind me and witnessed fifty-plus young people standing. Both Cheryls brought souls to The Most High; it was awesome! Cheryl was crowned in heaven and big Cheryl definitely will be when she gets there.

After the guests left, my family stayed behind to have more alone time with Cheryl. I ran my fingers through her hair, placed my hand on her arm and kissed her cheek, telling her "I love you. I thank YAH for allowing me to be your mother."

My children kissed her, saying their final sweet good-byes also. It was so very hard for us to walk away from her.

When Pastor Allen said, "It's time," then I knew it was okay. There was not to be a procession to the cemetery due to the fact that Veterans cemeteries had appointed times for their burial ceremonies. My ex-husband, her father, had been a veteran, so she was to be buried in the VA cemetery with her dad.

Everyone was outside waiting for us, so the doves could be released. I took a dove out, one by one, counting as each dove represented a year of Cheryl's life. Before the funeral director left, he whispered to me, "I have over-seen many funerals, but never felt the peace as I did here today."

The after-passing, or the repast, was immediately held across the street in a building the church owned. As we ate together, peace, love, and support flowed through everyone. Approximately four hundred people attended Cheryl's funeral, including family, friends and unknown supporters.

Season Five

Willing and Ready

Returning home was a relief. I got much needed quietness for myself. I went to my bedroom for prayer, asking YAHWEH for guidance, knowing I must still move forward in bringing peace and unity for the community.

Early morning, I rose in prayer. "God cover me and my family, continue to give me strength, and allow Your Holy Spirit to guide me." Later that morning, the detectives called, saying they needed to talk with me and that they will be here shortly.

I heard knocking at my front door. It was the neighbors showing me today's *Los Angeles Times* newspaper and on the front page was titled *"Farewell to Teen,"* with a large picture of Cheryl lying in her casket. I had mixed emotions about seeing the picture; however, it was necessary. I wanted the world to know the pain that this gang has caused several families of that community.

When the detectives arrived, I welcomed them in. We sat at the usual place as they began to tell me more about the investigation.

They searched more homes, finding evidence such as weapons, ammunition, and racial epithet-swastika signs on their walls.

"It was unbelievable," said Detective Falvo. "More arrests have been made, and we have more information about the shooter."

They asked me did I find a new place to relocate to, and I replied, "No." They advised me to do so "quickly!"

I was deeply concerned, thinking it's something they're not telling me. I shared what the detectives told me to my family. We then prayed, asking YHWH, "To protect and cover us from seen and unseen danger." In the midst of everything, I started looking for a new place for my family to live.

I spoke with Najee about the town hall meeting being held at 6 o'clock that evening and that I would be attending. When I arrived, the place was full of concerned citizens from the community, agents from the Los Angeles police department, Human Relations Commission Officials, Gang Interventionists, and Councilwoman Hahn, (who later became a US congresswoman). Everyone came with different agendas in mind; however, promoting the same solution for the problem. The residents asked for a gang injunction.

A gang-injunction is to prevent gang-members from congregating together in public and for minor violations, it would impose penalties. We also asked for more police patrol in the neighborhood. Human Relations officials talked about uniting the community, teaching better race relations in school, and creating anti-gang programs.

The Deputy City Attorney said, "This matter will be getting the utmost attention. Also, the gang-injunction is already in process."

Councilwoman Hahn said, "This kind of tragic shooting of Cheryl is not acceptable. It should break the heart of every one of us. I am upset and I'm angry. I feel a little bit guilty that this has been allowed to continue in this neighborhood until we lost a young girl."

She also talked about increasing patrol, and the gang-injunction for the neighborhood.

Linda Mayner, a playground supervisor from the elementary school Cheryl graduated from, said that Black students, ages 7 and 8, told her that they stayed after school to play because they feared playing outside their homes.

I hoped from the meeting that it would make a complete change for the neighborhood, that we no longer would live in fear.

Season Six

Manifested Faith

January 1st, I stayed inside, lying in my bed. At night, I listened to all the gun shots that scared me, then angered me at the same time.

January 4th, 2007. I'd been invited to appear on a local Christian television program with Melvin. Five minutes before filming, my cell phone rang. It was Detective Falvo, saying the sweetest sounding words a murdered child's mother longs to hear. "WE GOT HIM!

"We captured the shooter last night and he confessed."

I lifted my hands to YAH and replied, "Praise God, Praise God.

"Thank you so much, Detective."

After talking with him, I lifted my hands again to YHWH and gave Him all praise and the Glory with full thankfulness in my heart. (Readers, I want you to know God is **Real** and **Alive**. YHWH is the **Creator,** I **believe** this with every **breath** that I **breathe**). He is miraculous and amazing in everything He has done, He is doing and will do!

Later that evening, it was on every news channel. "The shooter has been captured." I received phone calls from family and friends with praise and thankfulness about the Victorious victory.

Marching Through

The following day, my family, Najee and Melvin, Councilwoman Hahn, residents and other politicians of nearby cities gathered together for a peace march. We held another press conference in front of the apartment building where I lived, addressing the media to talk about our mission and the purpose of the march. We were going to introduce ourselves to the neighbors on 204th Street, who out of fear, never ventured past the "Invisible line." It also was to promote a mentoring program so that Blacks and Latinos could learn about the different cultures of each other to understand one another. More importantly, to take a stand against this gang of detestation and racism.

We started the march from my apartment building at 1638 W. 207th Street, heading west to Western Blvd. Then we headed north, passing 206th and 205th Street, chanting, "Peace and Unity for the Community," until we reached 204th Street. Some neighbors looked out their windows and doors, while others came out to talk and walk with us.

One particular Latina caught my attention. Councilwoman Hahn and myself walked over to her and told her our names and who we were. I told her my daughter Cheryl was the young girl who was killed on December 15th.

I proceeded to ask her, "How old are you and what do you want to be when you grow up?"

She responded, "I'm fourteen. I want to be a Veterinarian when I grow up."

"I love animals, that's a great profession. Follow your dream."

I was so in the moment, I didn't consider the questions I asked—knowing my 14-year-old daughter would never grow up and would never live out her dreams.

After talking with some of the Hispanic neighbors, we continued up 204th Street until we reached the "off-limit," Del Amo Market that the gang claimed as their own. Before entering, I received an uneasy feeling because in my six years of living in the Harbor Gateway neighborhood I had never been inside the market. We went in chanting "Peace and Unity for the Community."

While inside, some of the people actually purchased items from the market. It was a major accomplishment and an abundant fulfillment crossing the **"Invisible line."**

We continued on from 204th Street to Harbor Blvd, the street Cheryl was killed on, marching to 206th Street to the driveway where she died. Everyone stood looking at the candles, balloons, stuffed animals, and candy people left at the memorial. As we marched back to 207th Street, we finished yelling our slogan, "PEACE and UNITY for the COMMUNITY."

Letters and a Poem

I heard a knock at the front door and got up to answer it. I was surprised because it was Cheryl's English teacher, Ms. Cox. I welcomed her in and we sat down at the dining room table. She handed me a letter and a poem that Cheryl wrote a month prior. With empathy she told me how sorry she was to hear about the loss of Cheryl as she began to cry. She expressed how much she enjoyed having Cheryl in her class. I read the letter and in it she expressed how she observed Cheryl progress from seventh to eighth grade and how she evolved from a shy girl to a young lady of maturity and curiosity, who never said an unkind word in her class. The letter also explained that Cheryl was one of her students who grew strong academically and often would get the best grade on her grammar tests.

At the end of the letter, she wrote, "Cheryl was absolutely a true pleasure to have in class. She made me want to teach.

"Most importantly, she was a good human being with a pure heart—it was my fortune to know Cheryl Green."

Then I read Cheryl's poem titled, *"I Am."* "I am black and beautiful."

"I wonder how I will be living in the future."

In the poem, she describes different emotions and thoughts, but after every fifth line she wrote, "I am black and beautiful." The poem was an epiphany to me. It seemed to me as if Cheryl knew she would not be here with us much longer. However, the poem was categorically beautiful! She used different color markers as if she was making a rainbow with her writing.

To Ms. Cox, I was deeply touched and highly thankful for her taking the time to find where we lived and bring me what I feel is priceless! I hugged her tightly before leaving. (Later, the coincidence of Cheryl's poem revealed the bigger picture.) For Cheryl to have written a poem prior to her death titled, "I Am," and the theme of it was "I'm Black and Beautiful," it gave me a thought. Maybe she herself had a premonition and knew her death would bring a positive change to the community.

The next day, I received a letter in the mailbox from the previous tenant named Toni, who lived in the apartment prior to my move in. I opened it and could see the dried teardrops on the paper. She wrote how sorry she was for not telling me about the killing of Black people in the neighborhood when I came to inquire about the apartment. She was mournfully apologetic in her writing as she also stated how she was one of the nurses who tried to help revive Cheryl at Harbor UCLA hospital. She felt responsible, thinking if she would have told me I would have not moved my family there. She included her phone number, so . I called her. I thanked her for the letter, but told her that it was not her fault. She was not responsible for the gang and their hate.

She said, "If there is anything—anything at all I can do, please let me know."

I thanked her again before hanging up the phone. (It was another moment, I realized God's plan was in effect).

After all the local news stations heard about the tragedy of Cheryl death, many journalists from the different news stations wanted to make appointments to interview me and I agreed. The shooting and death of my daughter made national headlines. The world finally knew about the racism that was hidden in the city of Harbor Gateway.

I began getting e-mails and phone calls from concerned people around the world. A journalist named Randal Archibold, a National Correspondent from *The New York Times,* phoned and asked could he come interview me. I agreed.

On January 13th, 2007, days later, he arrived, and the interview was done. Later, I received a phone call from Congresswoman, Maxine Waters, giving me her condolences and support. I got an e-mail from a mother living in Jersey, who shared with me about a burglary at her home, which lead to the murder of her daughter. Her daughter had an intimate relationship with God; however, the mother didn't believe in Him. The daughter kept urging her mother to believe. After her daughter was killed, she began seeking God. She heard about the death of Cheryl and the amazing things YAH was doing in the midst of my pain. My story was her inspiration. She became a believer of GOD ALL MIGHTY.

Children Calling for Peace

On January 13, 2007, the students from 186th Elementary School had a peace march in honor of Cheryl. She was once their fellow classmate, before graduating to middle school. The students marched around, holding their posters, promoting peace. During the march, the principal, Marcia Reed, spoke about Dr. Martin Luther King's message of nonviolence. She told the students to go home and talk with their parents about peace.

After her speech, fifty doves were released, circling over the school before returning back home. It was absolutely amazing!

The following day Harbor Blvd was blocked off between 207th and 206th Street, where Cheryl was slain. Residents, activists, politicians and the Mayor of Los Angeles, Antonio Villaraigosa, came out for a rally to discuss solutions to gang violence. When I arrived, Mayor Villaraigosa walked up to me and gave me his condolences. Before the rally began, we had a moment of prayer.

Villaraigosa talked about how the community must stand together to fight against the gangs. "We will do all we can to prevent, intervene and help, but to those who do harm to others, particularly innocent victims, you should know they will be asked to pay the consequences. We are here to show them that violence will not be tolerated," he continued. He declared gang crime "Public Enemy No.1," and that several approaches were being pursued.

Councilwoman Hahn spoke about how she and I went door-to-door to meet the neighbors on 204th Street and that they were afraid to open their doors. She shared with the people how one Latina woman peeked out of her door, but when we told her that I was the mother of the 14-year-old girl who was killed a few weeks ago, she welcomed us in.

"We have to take back our neighborhoods," Hahn said. "It can be done."

Residents, Black and Latino, told their own ideas on how to end the cycle of violence. Our ideas included 1) Build a community center, 2) improve the lighting on the streets and 3) increase police patrol. The atmosphere was pessimistic but, some residents feared they would just forget about the problem and it will go back to the same ole thing.

We held a press conference in front of the market that Blacks were not allowed to patronize. It was another one of our strategies to get all agencies to help end the racism and killing in the neighborhood.

As a result of the press conference we had, two days later, Mayor Villaraigosa, and a host of federal and law enforcement officials, held a press conference in front of the "off- limits" market. They united their forces to subdue the Harbor Gateway gang.

Mayor Villaraigosa announced, "You heard it here first today. We're here to say that we're putting the 204th Street gang out of business."

Then, Police Chief William Bratton of Los Angeles spoke, saying, "Spread the word.

We are not coming—we are here. We're more united than ever— we're not messing around this time."

Councilwoman Hahn took her turn in addressing the media. "We cannot incarcerate our way out of this problem." She talked about intervention and

prevention that will stop kids from wanting to join gangs by having more after-school programs, creating recreational centers and community conversing sessions.

The City Attorney, Rocky Delgadillo, revealed that the gang injunction would be imposed in the area within a few months.

The Mayor closed the press conference, saying, "No one should have to fear for their life because of the color of their skin, not in our city, not in our county."

It felt good knowing the press conference we held grabbed the attention needed to help make that neighborhood a safe place to live.

In addition to the press conference, the Los Angeles Police Department and the Carson Sheriff's Department became partners. In every county, there are police departments that protect that particular county, and would not pass into other jurisdictions; however, since the nation-wide media coverage of Cheryl, it changed the old into anew! Both departments working together modeled for other counties how to help each other in stopping gang activities and other crimes.

Within everything taking place, I did find a safe place for my family to live. We moved into our new home on February 1st, 2007 (Hallelujah). It was bitter sweet, we had been a part of the community for six years. I expressed to everyone we're moving, but we will continue to do what's necessary to make it safe for "All" to live in this neighborhood. My work here is not finished.

Season Seven

Double and Grace

We moved into our three-bedroom home on the corner of Double and Grace Street in Carson, California, relieved to be in a safe environment. The residents on the street seem to have lived in the neighborhood for a lengthy time. It was well-kept and very quiet. I played bingo at the church, which was towards the other end of the street. That's how I found the house. We were excited about our move and felt free.

A week after settling in, my oldest daughter came into the living-room and sat beside me on the sofa. She looked at me and said, "Mommy, I'm pregnant." I could not believe what I was hearing.

"You too? How many weeks are you?"

She responded, "Six weeks."

I knew the answer to the next question was "Yes," so I didn't ask, but I surely was over-whelmed! Wow, two grandbabies on the way! A few days later, I walked outside, stood on the porch and stared at the street signs putting the names together. It read to me "Double Grace."

YAH is awesome, giving me double blessings at one time, knowing those grandbabies would give me the love needed to continue on.

It was the 10th of February, 2007, when I get a phone call from Najee about a racial attack from a group of Blacks on three Latinas in Inglewood as they walked home from school, which was totally unacceptable. Najee and I decided to join in on the unity rally in Inglewood for the following day. It was organized by Latino 96.3 FM, "The Morning Show, The Latino and African-American Leadership Alliance."

The day of the "Unity Rally," we joined hands for prayer of peace and racial acceptance before marching around Inglewood's City Hall. The media was there to capture our demonstration, as we chanted, "The people united can never be divided," which was said in English and Spanish. The three Latinas that were assaulted, one with a fat lip and the other with a black eye, marched hand-in-hand with us. I was proud of them for having the courage to come out against racism. One of the victim's sister said, "We just need to get along."

A few days later the detectives came by to check on us. I was a little concerned because they kept asking, "Are you okay?"

"Yes," I said, "we're good. We like it here a lot."

They asked, "Are you sure?"

Reassuring them, I said, "Yes, we are fine."

"Okay," they said, "Give us a call if you need anything."

Another Innocent Victim

The detectives had reasons for concerns. Now I understand why they were so adamant about my family moving away from 207th

Street, and also why they were against the new location of where we moved. There was more tragedy to the story.

On December 28th, one day after Cheryl's funeral, Christopher Ash, an associate of the gang, was stabbed over eighty times and his throat was slashed. His body was dumped in the city of Carson where we had we just moved. Apparently, he was one of the gang members arrested during the search warrants, questioned and then released. The other gang-members thought he gave the police information on the killing of my daughter; however, detective Angus Fergus told that Ash didn't tell them anything. However, the five gang members that killed Ash, one of them was the murderer who killed my daughter.

Unexpected Recognition

I was asked to attend a formal award ceremonial dinner by Eric Lee, who is the President of the *Southern Christian Leadership Conference of Greater Los Angeles, California.* It was founded in 1957 in Montgomery, Alabama by church leaders. They brought all civil rights organizations under one umbrella and called it *Southern Christian Leadership Conferences.* Their concept is to handle all violent situations with non-violence. Dr. Martin Luther King, Jr. was elected President and was at the forefront of battling the horrific racism Blacks suffered in the 1950s-60s. The SCLC orchestrated the "March" on Washington, which made it possible for Blacks to vote. Also, they protested throughout the cities in the South bringing attention to the injustice of Blacks.

I talked with Najee about the invite to the dinner ceremony. He encouraged me to go saying, "It would be good. The more they see you, they will know you will not rest until changes have been made in Harbor Gateway," I agreed.

I was told I could bring 3 guests, so I chose my son David, my aunt Laura and Rachel, who had been very supportive during the many press conferences and interviews. Najee met us there.

After arriving, I met more concerned politicians and Leaders of different organizations. They gave me their condolences and business cards, saying if there was anything they could do to be of help, let them know. Consequently, I did reach out to Constance Rice, who is a conspicuous civil rights activist, also cousin of Condoleezza Rice, 66th Secretary of State. She became another supporter of my mission to help end racism in Harbor Gateway.

During the meet and greet, I saw Councilwoman Hahn. I thanked her again, letting her know how much I appreciated her and all the support she had given me and my family. I also had the opportunity to meet her mother who was very meek. I could see the sparkle in her eyes when she looked at her daughter; she was absolutely in awe of her.

We were given our seating arrangements and went to our table. Dinner was served and afterwards the award ceremony began. We applauded as each person received their award in their outstanding contributions to the County of Los Angeles.

Councilwoman Hahn was called to receive the Rosa Parks Award for her contribution in creating jobs, how she fought for wage increases, created after-school programs and job training. In doing so, kids can have an alternative to joining gangs. The many different acts of courage for Councilwoman Hahn goes on. They called Councilwoman Hahn to take her award. However, before giving her speech, she talked about Cheryl and myself. Then asked me to come up to the podium. She dedicated her award to me. I was wide-eyed and in awe of her, sharing this prestigious award with me. At first, I didn't move, but Najee nudged me to walk up there. Everyone stood and applauded as I made my way up to Councilwoman Hahn. I hugged her tightly with thanks-given, then holding hands while she gave her speech.

I received a letter in the mail from the Mayor's office titled, *Commission on the Status of Women*. It informed me that Councilwoman Hahn selected me to represent her District as the 2007 Pioneer Woman of the year, which would be held on March 30th, 2007. Women's History Month "Pioneer Women" are women who have contributed towards improving the community within her Council District and improving the status of women in the City of Los Angeles. She has participated and excelled in a nontraditional field, has also been involved in philanthropic endeavors, and have performed acts of courage.

The acknowledgments of my efforts to stop the evilness that plagued a community, stole the lives of innocent victims and horrified families, was a grand gesture, but it didn't take a moment to decide if I should—I was compelled to action.

Season Eight

In Between Time

In the meantime, I made sure my daughters set appointments for prenatal care and talked with the fathers, making sure they understood what I expected of them. They were young and beginning a life of parenthood. But both young men understood their role as fathers and have been ever present in their children's lives. Subsequently, both daughters have had an additional kid from the same fathers, which gives me a total of four grandkids, thus far (Ariana, Nigel Jr., Ni Sear and Jordan), they give me "laughter, love, joy and strength."

March

Najee phoned me to ask if I would be willing to have an interview with a journalist from *Essence* magazine. Once again, I was willing, continuing in telling my story. The changes in the neighborhood were not yet in full effect. Until then, I must, "March."

When the interview was published in August 2007, I was surprisingly stunned. I read an excerpt at the bottom of the page from a resolution passed in spring 2007 by the Alabama legislature apologizing for their role in slavery, "...an apology for centuries of brutal dehumanization and injustices cannot erase the past, but confession of the wrong can speed racial healing and reconciliation and help African-Americans, and White citizens confront the ghosts of their collective past together." Consequently, Maryland, Virginia and North Carolina modeled the same year. (WOW)

Another interview I did wasn't so pleasant. It was not the interviewer, but the information he came with. A journalist from the Sacramento Bee newspaper out of Washington asked me, "How did you feel about the comment Governor Arnold Schwarzenegger made?"

I knew nothing of what he was talking about until he showed me the article in the newspaper. Schwarzenegger said "people from all over the world live in harmony in California. We have a gang problem, but the girl's death didn't represent a larger problem in California." Then he added, "No matter which country you go to, you always have some instances like that, you know the Russian Mafia or some kind of gang violence in some country, or if it is soccer fans going crazy and trying to kill each other on the soccer field. You know there's crazy things all over the world."

I became so angry! I couldn't believe he compared my daughter's death to a soccer game and the Russian Mafia! I handed the journalist a picture of my baby lying in her casket and said, "Tell the governor, take a look at this picture and then talk to me about California living in peace and harmony."

In an article I read from the Sacramento Bee newspaper, the assembly members held a town hall meeting and collected anecdotes from communities around the state that showed Brown-on-Black crime was on the rise. The number one figure of hate crimes were towards African Americans, after the caucus released the State of California report. It also showed that racial violence was intensifying in the cities of Oakland, San Diego, Fresno, Santa Ana and Los Angeles, which required unified response.

I guess this goes along with the old saying, "It has to get worse, before it gets better." Even the prisons were having race-based riots between the Blacks and the Browns.

Days later, Najee phoned me. He wanted to know if I was interested in being part of a documentary called Gangland.

"Yes," I replied. I was committed to march forward with all my heart and soul to make a difference. The series of Gangland is to expose and highlight the different types of gangs, their activities and their territory throughout California.

We interviewed at my house in Carson. Afterwards, we drove to the previous address I lived at to capture the location and the neighborhood. From there we continued filming, walking to the driveway where Cheryl was murdered. I walked up to the exact spot where she was standing when gunned down.

I said to them, "Look the driveway is closed in. She was trapped— she had nowhere to run to for shelter." I began sobbing.

On the morning of March 30th, my mother and I arrived at City Hall for the Pioneer Women of the Year Breakfast Reception in the Tom Bradley Tower. Afterwards, we took the elevator down to the Award Presentation in the City Council Chambers. It was filled to capacity with the other awardees, and their family members, the

Council members and their staff, including the President of Council, Eric Garcetti and the mayor of Los Angeles.

I applauded as the women were recognized for their outstanding achievements in making their councilmember's district better. However, once again I had mixed emotions.

I was receiving this award because I chose not to let my daughter's death just be another statistic. Several innocent victims have lost their lives because of that gang and their hatred towards Blacks in that community, but nothing had been done to stop the killings. I couldn't and wouldn't let my daughter's death be in vain. I knew I had to stand up and allow GOD to use me to turn this tragedy into something good. It was not a choice for me. Ergo, it was my assignment!

It was Councilwoman Hahn's turn to give her award. She walked up to the podium, then motioned for me to come up. I walked up to her and she hugged me tightly. Clearing her throat before speaking she said, "Every year on this day we have to choose a woman from our district to be our pioneer woman. Every year we talk about it in my office. We often come up with suggestions and ask staff members who would be the best woman for our pioneer woman of the year. This year there was no discussion, this year there was no hesitation, this year I knew without a doubt who I wanted to honor as my pioneer woman of the year and I'm very pleased to present Ms. Charlene Lovett as my pioneer woman of the year." She also stated how Cheryl's death had become a national story.

Hahn talked about the door to door walk we did in the neighborhood and mentioned the conversation we had with the fourteen-year-old Latina, asking her, "What did she want to be when she grew up?" Knowing full well that my daughter would never grow up and become what she wanted to be, I was speechless.

Hahn went on to say, "In the midst of your pain, you made me a better woman. I've never met a woman like you in my whole life and I don't think I ever will."

"I first thanked YAHWEH, giving Him all honor, praise and glory. Then I thanked Councilwoman Hahn for being by my side, from the very first day I started my journey of this peace march." I held up the bow of the dress my daughter was buried in and said, "This is my baton right here. Every time you see me, you will see this. I am here for peace. I will continue in peace and I will do everything in my power that God gives me to promote peace in the City and the County of Los Angeles, thank you."

Making the Change

According to the *Daily Breeze*, changes are taking place. Law enforcement rounded up parole violators, made several arrests due to gang activity and passed out fliers to residents to report criminal gang activities. Also, Steven White Middle school where Cheryl was attending, expanded their after-school programs to give kids a refuge from gangs. Several schools added more subjects to their after-school programs, such as basketball teams, homework clubs and educational games. The Boys and Girls Club where Cheryl would attend after school, also stepped in helping students with homework and tutoring. (I will tell you later about the Boys and Girls Club, and how they honored Cheryl in an extraordinary way).

My children and I went to Steven White Middle School to attend a talent show they were giving in honor of Cheryl. It was absolutely beautiful. The students were in good spirits and gave wonderful performances. The principal walked over to me and said, "We still want to give Cheryl her diploma."

She asked would I walk the stage for her. My face lit up, "Yes, I will walk the stage for her." I was exceedingly happy and overjoyed!

June 13th, 2007, my children and I went to Cheryl's graduation ceremony. We were first greeted by the media with short interviews on how we felt about the day. It was again a situation where I had mixed emotions. Cheryl was not here to accept her own diploma; however, I was proud to be there in her place to receive it. Once inside where the ceremony was being held, we were greeted by her classmates and other students with hugs and fond memories of Cheryl. The teachers also greeted us with hugs and told their stories too. Cheryl was popular at school because of her bubbly personality and the love that flowed from her heart, her kindness and her humility.

After we took our seats, the principal spoke encouraging words to the graduating students. Then the graduating class went up with their teacher to receive their diplomas. When Cheryl's class went up, I stayed seated in my chair until they called her name. I walked up full of energy, feeling Cheryl's presence and yelled, "Yeah, we did it."

Everyone clapped and had smiles on their faces. I gave a little speech telling the students, "There will be a negative situation in your life when you will have to make a choice on how to handle it. I asked that you choose peace. The outcome is always better." Then I yelled, "Congratulations," to all the graduating classes.

In the 2006-2007 yearbook, the school dedicated a page to Cheryl and titled it, "Our Fallen Knight." After the ceremony, Cheryl's classmates and other students came up to me so they could autograph her yearbook.

The following month, I received a letter from the *County of Los Angeles Commission On Human Relations and the Board of Supervisors.* I had been selected by Don Knabe, who is supervisor over the Fourth District, to receive the John Anson Ford Award titled, "Celebrating Our Unity," on October 24th at the Millennium Biltmore Hotel downtown Los Angeles. The Commission Human Relations started back in January 1944 by Supervisor John Anson Ford and Executive Director John Allen Buggs in the Zoot Suit era, there were riots and conflicts between them and other groups of people.

The Commission Human Relations were fruitful in constructing greater levels of common understanding and resolutions of conflicts in an inter-racial crisis. Together with devoted citizens they set the foundation and moved forward with open-mindedness to seek brotherhood and harmony for all people.

I was flattered by the recognition and looked forward to the event.

Birth Days-Bundles of Joy

It was August 19th, Cheryl's birthday. We preplanned a birthday celebration for her at a luxury hotel ballroom in the neighborhood where we lived previously. The neighbors that wanted to celebrate with us were there along with other activists. I was amazed to know that Cesar Chavez's granddaughter, Christine Chavez, came to celebrate and support the cause of uniting Black and Brown. Cesar Chavez, who in his early life, worked with The Community Service to bring people together of all ethnicities to identify and solve problems in their community. He became an activist representing people across California. He followed Dr. Martin Luther King Jr.'s strategy by handling all situations with nonviolence. His granddaughter grew up to follow in her grandfather's footsteps.

The media was there because I continuously wanted Cheryl's story told.

On August 25th, I celebrated the new arrival of Ariana Spencer, then six weeks later on October 13th, 2007, the second new arrival of Nigel Key, Jr, my grandbabies! They bring me so much joy and the overflowing love I have for them is unexplainable. I am truly "double blessed." As they grew, it was so amazing to see characteristics of their aunty Cheryl in them. YAH is awesome, allowing us to have some of Cheryl's attributes here still with us.

Uneasy Feelings

In the midst of it all, I kept feeling uncomfortable about where we moved to, knowing that the man who supposedly snitched body was dumped in Carson. I decided to move my family again. This time the location was nowhere near the two cities we previous lived. That uneasiness I felt was not revealed to me until the trial. The revelation was shocking!

We moved into our new place, feeling absolutely refreshed!

October 24th was the day of the "Celebrating Our Unity" Award Luncheon, but unfortunately, I was not physically up to it. My spirit was willing, but my body was weak. I had been on a fast track since the day Cheryl was killed. I had moved twice in a year, and it finally caught up to me physically. I was disappointed with myself for not attending; however, I needed to nurse myself and get well. My mission was not over!

Marching forward, we continued to bring peace and unity to the Harbor Gateway community. In December 2007, a week before Cheryl's 1st year memorial, Najee and I went to Harbor Gateway to pass out fliers, letting the residents know we were having a "Peace and Unity" candle-light vigil in remembrance of Cheryl.

On December 15th my family, Najee, Councilwoman Hahn, activists and politicians met with residents in the driveway where Cheryl was killed. Councilwoman Hahn announced that there had been land donated to the neighborhood from The Department of Water and Power and The Boys and Girls Club will be putting a center there in her honor as a memorial for Cheryl. After hearing the announcement, we all were overjoyed. There will be a place for kids to come together (Blessing from above). Big Cheryl led a prayer, asking for peace love and unity to forever be present in Harbor-Gateway. It was powerful!

On November 26th, 2008, the day before Thanksgiving and seven days before my birthday, my third grandbaby was born, Nisear Key! No other gift would be greater! I took time spending it with my beautiful grandbabies, savoring every moment. They are truly blessings in my life. No one could ever take the place of my Cheryl; however, The Most High sent me grandkids to love and to keep me busy. The love I get from each one of them puts a smile on my face.

THE OPENING

June 15th, 2009 was the day of the ribbon cutting for The Boys & Girls Club Harbor Gateway/ Torrance Cheryl Green Youth Center.

Before the ceremony I walked to the lettering on the wall and started crying. I was overjoyed, yet still mourned that it was the death of my baby is how this youth center came into existence.

The ceremony started. Councilwoman Hahn gave a speech about how we talked in the past about having somewhere safe in the neighborhood for the kids. For two-and-a- half years, Hahn used all her resources and networking until she got what we wanted. The Boys & Girl Club knew that Cheryl was one of their members and immediately was willing to help. Many companies from the South Bay area donated work with hundreds of residents helping with gardening painting and pouring concrete. The center also is a place where students can come after school for tutoring, computer work, and to learn how to speak English and Spanish for children and parents. People can donate food, clothes, and hold community meetings there also.

It was a beautiful sight to see! Black and Hispanic kids jump roping, doing arts and crafts together, while parents took turns barbequing hamburgers and hotdogs. I thought back a couple of years, when random people knocked on my door, trying to get the okay from me to avenge Cheryl's death and I told them no! I knew if I kept the faith and continued to follow in His path, He would turn this tragedy into something truly wonderful and amazing. When I glanced around, I felt Cheryl's spirit. For me, it was undeniably a magnificent and breathtaking moment.

Season Nine

The Trial-Two in One

It was 2010, midsummer. I received a phone call from Deputy District Attorney Gretchen Ford, asking if I would come to her office and bring any special effects that I had of Cheryl, such as pictures, poems, holiday cards, Mother's Day cards, etc. So a couple days later, I met with Mrs. Ford and brought the things she asked for. She explained to me that she would be the prosecutor, representing Cheryl's case. She told me that we were ready to move forward with the beginning of trial. A court date was set to start jury selection, but there was no need for me to attend; she would call me to let me know the actual date of the trial.

In the beginning of August, I received the phone call with a trial date, which would be on the 11th of August. I called my children on their cell phone and said, "We've been waiting. It's going on five years, but finally we have a court date."

I gave them the date, time, and what court building the trial would be held. I then called my mom and gave her the same information. My mother, my oldest daughter, Vanessa, and I decided we would ride together to the trial. My son, David, was still dealing with Cheryl's death and would not attend any court dates. I didn't want to take any chances with him getting extracted from the court room or being held in contempt. Allena, my second daughter, would attend on days she had a sitter for my granddaughter. No noise such as hollering, emotional out cries, or threats would be tolerated inside the courtroom.

However, I failed on the very first day. On August 11th, 2010 in the morning we walked into courtroom 102 and took our seats. I noticed a Hispanic female in her early twenties holding a girl toddler. As we walked to take seats in the first row of the courtroom, the deputy stopped us.

"These seats are for lawyers and detectives only."

We sat in front of the Hispanic lady. Court did not start until thirty minutes later, by now we figured out the Hispanic lady and toddler was there for the defendant. She was the mother of his daughter.

Finally, the judge walked out of a door facing us on the right side of his desk. Then from the opposite side the jurors walked out of the door and took their seats. The right side door to the courtroom opened. Walking through the door was the killer of Cheryl in an orange jumpsuit. He looked past me and fixed his eyes on the girlfriend and child. He was happy. He acted as if no one else was inside the courtroom. I want to think it was the first time he saw his daughter because she was pregnant at the time he murdered my child (what's the irony of that).

My eyes stayed on him as he took his seat facing the judge. I kept my eyes on him as he looked back every few seconds admiring his daughter. Then he finally realized who I was, the mother of the child he killed. His face went blank as he turned forward and squinted his eyes. I had no feeling, no emotions and absolutely no fear regarding him. Ergo, I stood strong, confident, full of faith about what The Most High revealed to me what shall come to past.

The right side door to the courtroom opened for a second time and another male Hispanic with an orange jumpsuit walked through and was seated next to the first inmate. He was one of the men that helped kill Christopher Ash, the so-called snitch. Turns out the other four men involved in killing him told on each other, and had to be tried separately. The reason these two were able to be tried together is because the second defendant had nothing to do with Cheryl's murder, but the two of them with other gang members were together when killing Christopher Ash. "The Watchman" of Cheryl's killer will be judged at a later date; he became state's evidence for the prosecuting side.

District Attorney Ford began her opening statements, telling jurors they will see evidence and hear testimonies about the gang's hatred towards Blacks. Ford then told about the so-called morning events that led up to the shooting and the death of my daughter. According to what she said, the morning of December 15th, 2006, Cheryl's killer and some of his acolytes were at the Del Amo Market (their hangout place) and approached a Black male sitting inside his car. The man pulled out a gun and they ran.

The defendant went to Christopher Ash's house and retrieved a .44 caliber revolver, which he had stashed under his couch. He and the watchman went to the location where Cheryl and her friends were standing and began firing. However, there was no evidence found about a Black male at the market, nor any testimonies, but the shooting and death of Cheryl was to get more notoriety and to further enhance their gang.

Ford also explained during weeks after the shooting, detectives served several search warrants, and on December 21st, 2006, they entered Ash's home where they found Ash and his best friend (second defendant) inside the home. During their search they found a modeled grenade. Police evacuated the home, arrested Ash and the second defendant. Afterwards, the gang got suspicious of Ash being released so quickly. They believed he snitched about the shooting and the death of Cheryl so they devised a plan to kill him.

The second defendant, being Ash's best friend, was used to lure Ash to another gang - member's house and into the garage. The first defendant hit Ash in the head with a shotgun. Then the other gang members took turns stabbing him, in which he suffered more than eighty stabs and his throat was slashed. Afterwards, they dumped his body in the city of Carson.

Earlier I told you about the uneasy feeling I had living in Carson. After hearing about Ash's death and where they dumped his body, I understood why. I lived in a corner house in Carson. When I walked out my house I could look north or south and see several streets down. When looking north, three streets down there's a dead end. That's exactly where they discarded his body. It was almost unreal to hear; however, now it made sense to me why I felt the way I did. Also, why the detectives were still so concerned about where I had moved my family.

Finally, Ford said she would play a recording of Cheryl's killer admitting he killed her.

The defense attorneys took their turn with opening statements, stating the second defendant knew nothing about killing Ash, but did kick him once or twice after he was dead. The reason he participated with the gang was only out of fear.

For the first defendant, he admitted to shooting the gun and killing Cheryl, but it was an accident.

Court stopped for an hour and a half for lunch, and yes, it was much needed. Listening to the opening statements was overwhelming! However, that was nothing compared to what's about to take place once back in-session.

Returning from lunch, we entered back into the courtroom and took our same seats. The same sequence of the morning was done again. The judge, defendants, and then the jurors all came out and took their seats. Court was back in-session.

Ford called Anthony Buckner to take the witness stand. She began to question him about what took place on December 15th, 2006 at 3:10 that afternoon. Buckner fixed his eyes on the shooter/ murderer and told how him, his cousins, and Cheryl was standing inside their driveway (the more he told what happened, the angrier he got, not taking his eyes off the defendant), when they saw the defendant walk up, point his gun at him and his little cousin he was holding in his arms. He pulled the trigger, but the gun jammed. Then he pointed the gun towards Cheryl and fired several times.

While listening to Buckner's testimony, tears started rolling down my face. Then he said once the shooter stopped shooting, he ran. Buckner went over to Cheryl where she was lying on the ground, and as he was trying to pick her up, her eyes were looking up with tears in them. I couldn't hold it in any longer. I started sobbing to the point that the judge stopped the session and called Mrs. Ford to the bench.

The judge advised her to talk with me about crying out loud because the defendant's attorneys could call for a mistrial, thinking I could persuade the jurors in my favor with empathy. She then went back inside the courtroom. I was angry for a moment, thinking how they can expect me to hear the last moments of my child's life and not react the way I did! I composed myself and returned back inside the courtroom.

Mrs. Ford was whispering to Buckner and his reply was, "It's hard not to look at him." He put his face in his hands and started sobbing. He ended his testimony, telling the jurors that he and his cousin, who was not wounded, had a hard time putting Cheryl inside his car. She was heavy, and he believed she was already gone.

Ford asked Buckner, "Is the person that pointed a gun at you, shot your cousins and killed Cheryl Green in the courtroom today, and if so, will you point at him?"

Buckner said, "Yes," and pointed at the defendant (one). When Buckner was told he could leave from the witness stand, he slammed the door behind himself. It made the judge warn everyone inside the courtroom that no emotions or displays of anger would be tolerated. "You will be ejected from the courtroom or arrested."

Several more testimonies were given by the other victims. They gave the same account as Buckner; however, the mother of the little boy, apparently who is older now, did not want her son to be questioned at all. I understood her concern, but I knew it was important for the prosecutor to get his statement, so I went out to talk with his mother. She was adamant that she was not letting her son get on the witness stand, explaining to me the therapy he endured because of this and that he was just now starting to get back to being unafraid. After she told me that, I pulled back with complete understanding. I would have done the same for my child. Instead, I prayed for her and her son.

After praying, she asked if it was possible for her to take the stand in his place? I told her to let me talk with Mrs. Ford. After doing so, she was called to the witness stand (how Great YAH is). Ford asked her what did she know about the shooting that took place on December 15th, 2006. The witness explained to her what was told to her by her little cousins.

Ford then asked, "What effects did it have on her son after the incident?"

She told Ford that she moved from the location where the incident took place and how her son had been in therapy up until the beginning of 2010. She stated that's why she didn't want her son to take the witness stand. Returning from the witness stand, she said to me, "That was it? I wanted her to ask me more!"

Day after day, we went into courtroom 102 and heard testimonies, and day after day, I went in hoping to see if this murderer would show remorse, not for me—but for himself!

Today, Detective Falvo took the stand and told how during the raid, they found guns, bullets, swastika symbols and drug paraphernalia. He also told about the audio recording of defendant one admitting to killing Cheryl. Mrs. Ford then played the recording for the jurors to hear him confessing to the shooting and killing my baby. At the end of the recording the detectives left out of the interrogation room and the defendant started singing a song about his 44 Glock, (gun). I could not believe what I was hearing!

August 17th, the gang member that copped a deal with the prosecutors, who was involved in killing Ash, was called to the witness stand to testify against both defendants. This witness was already incarcerated and given his sentence of 22 years in state prison for the testimony he was about to give.

He told how it was decided by all men involved to kill Ash because he snitched about the killing of the girl. Defendant (two) brought Ash to their friend's house and as they went inside the garage, defendant (one) hit him in the head with a shotgun. Then someone stabbed him. He continued telling what happened and admitted to stabbing him, but while doing so he began to throw-up. He stabbed Ash again and threw up a second time. After Ash was dead, that's when defendant (two) kicked him once or twice.

The Public Defender questioned the witness and asked him at the time of killing Ash, "Is it true that you were dating Ash's sister?" he responded, "Yes."

Also, the Public Defender asked, "You admit to participating in the stabbing of Christopher Ash?"

He said, "Yes," again.

Then the defendant's lawyer asked, "Is it also true that after killing Ash, you returned back to Ash's home, got in bed with his sister, and went to sleep?"

"Yes," the witness said.

Finally, the Public Defender asked, "After the victim's mother and sister heard that Ash was killed, did you console them for their loss?"

Again, the witness said, "Yes."

My mother and I looked at each other and shook our heads in disbelief.

The defendant's lawyers knew they did not have a case against the prosecutors; they only questioned witnesses they thought they could discredit. The following day the killer of Cheryl came to court with two black eyes and a bruised lip. The prosecutors and defense lawyers were having a side-bar with the judge. Defendant one was in a fight with a deputy, so they had to have a mini trial for the assault.

I thought to myself, "WOW, he really is a Menace to Society!"

After the mini-trial, prosecutors called Detective Ferguson to the stand to give his testimony about apprehending the inmate that just gave testimony about killing Ash. Ferguson tells how the inmate confessed that all men involved in killing Ash did agree he had to be killed; it's regulation of their gang when you snitch.

August 19th, Cheryl's birthday. I knew it was going to be extremely hard for me to sit in the courtroom. I believe it was hard for everyone (except the defendant). They all knew it was her birthday; however, in my opinion, it gave them an unwavering desire to see this murderer get all what was coming to him. I prayed for strength because, if any day, this was the day I wanted to show "ALL" my emotions and, as if things couldn't get any tougher, the medical examiner was brought in to discuss and show pictures of the injuries and wounds. Also, the cause of death of Cheryl and Christopher Ash.

The prosecutor showed the medical examiner a picture of Christopher Ash's lifeless body at the location where he was found. When she asked the medical examiner questions, I watched the defendant (one) as he stared at the picture, looking at it as though he was seeing something he didn't take part in. To me, it seemed like he mentally disassociated himself from the killing of Ash and what was taking place in the courtroom. Then, Mrs. Ford questioned about the cuts on the body. The examiner told how they were defense wounds; however, the stabs injured him seriously, but the slashing of his throat was the final cause of his demise.

Mrs. Ford paused for a moment and walked over to me. She whispered in my ear that she was going to ask questions and show pictures of Cheryl. She suggested   I wait outside the courtroom. I thought about what she said for a moment and walked out the courtroom. Thank GOODNESS, none of my children were there because they might have stayed inside to hear and see what was said and shown. It was best for me not to have seen or heard that testimony. I know if I would have seen those pictures of my baby lying on the medical examiner's table, that image would have stayed forever in my memory. I am thankful she considered my feelings! I still have the imagery of Cheryl beautifully resting—peacefully.

The defendant's lawyers took their turn calling witnesses to the stand and with that being said, they absolutely had no defense. They called a psychologist to ask questions about the way the defendant was raised. Presuming it could have had an effect on his thought process. "Yes," he said, but not to the extent of committing murder.

I was thinking to myself in that case most humankind would be murderers. There's more poverty-stricken people in the world than there are rich.

Next, a gang expert was called to the stand, which turned in our favor. They absolutely had no defense! Almost everyone they called to the witness stand turned in favor of the prosecutor. The defendant's lawyers knew their clients were guilty; however, they were the Public Defenders chosen to represent them. The law states that anyone accused of a crime must be proven guilty in a criminal trial, under the Universal Declaration of Human Rights, article 11. They both confessed; however, neither pleaded guilty so there had to be a trial. Nonetheless, before the trial was over, defendant (one) pulled his last and final act.

It was the last week of trial. My mother, my daughter and I walked inside the courtroom. Once again, the prosecutors and defendant's lawyers were in a side bar with the judge. After talking with the judge there was another mini trial for defendant (one). When the defendant went through the metal detector it beeped. After checking him several times and not finding what was alerting the detector, they strip searched him. This menace had made a generic handcuff key and placed it inside the foreskin of his penis. We could not believe what the prosecutors was telling the judge.

By looking at all the faces in the courtroom, I want to think it was the first time anyone had heard of such a bizarre act like that. Again, more charges were added on to his case. Before the verdict, the prosecutors told us immediately after the verdict we would have to go through the penalty phase and be called to the witness stand to give testimonies on how the death of Cheryl impacted our lives. I was also asked by the prosecutors to bring treasurable sentiments of Cheryl's for the penalty phase to show jurors.

THE VERDICT

On August 24, 2010, the jury was instructed, the bailiff was sworn in to take charge of the jury, and deliberations began. Before leaving for the day, the jury was admonished not to talk, discuss, read, or look at any news coverage pertaining to the trial and was ordered to return on September 9, 2010. The jury returned and continued deliberating. At 12:00 p.m., they took a lunch break and returned back at 1:40 p.m. By 2:00 p.m., they had reached a verdict. Shortly before 3:00 p.m., the jurors walked into the courtroom. Previously, on court days, no juror would look my way. I believe they were instructed not to, nor be influenced by any of my emotions. This time some of them looked at me, but kept a blank face as they took their seat.

Then the judge asked the foreman, "Have you all reached a verdict?"

She answered, "Yes, we, the jury, find Defendant #1, guilty!"

Then she began reading all 9 accounts separately, all with special circumstances! Seven attempted murders of Nicole Buckner, Isadream Sims, Donald Rucker, Andre West, Anthony Buckner, Necharda Jones and Kenny Davis. His acts of violence were committed willfully, were deliberate and premeditated and found to be true.

The murders of Cheryl Green killed because of the color of her skin and murdered Christopher Ash thinking he snitched. Defendant #1 plotted and intentionally killed him. Special Circumstances was added in this case because defendant #1 carried out his horrific acts to further his gang credibility and bring more notoriety to his street gang, also committing a hate crime.

As she read the verdicts, my eyes stayed on the defendant, hoping I would see some kind of remorse. *Show me something,* I was thinking! Let me see that you feel bad—sorrowful for killing my baby! He just sat there blank faced and detached from what was going on inside the courtroom. Oh, but next week! He definitely will see things clearer than ever! Afterwards, the jury was polled to see if everyone agreed and the answer was "yes!'

When the jurors returned back inside the jury room, Mrs. Gretchen talked with me and said, "We're now at the last step, the penalty phase which will determine his sentence." She asked me to give her relatives' names who would be willing to give testimonies to the jury about Cheryl and how her death affected their lives. Also, the memorabilia of Cheryl and pictures I gave prior would be used at the penalty phase.

The judge gave the jury a week off before the last and final step, which was much needed for all of us. I thanked Mrs. Gretchen several times, telling her how much I appreciated her for everything she had done for us. I knew she was just doing her job, but I also knew she was especially picked-- from THE MOST HIGH. We hugged each other before departing.

While we had the week off from court I decided to buy thank-you cards and some keep-sakes. I inserted pictures of Cheryl and me to give to the prosecuting team and the lead detectives when we returned back to court.

On September 13th, my mom, my aunt Laura, my cousin, Veronica Davis, my oldest daughter, Vanessa, and I returned back to court together. When we entered the courtroom, I introduced my aunt and cousin to Mrs. Ford. My cousin was too emotional, so she did not give a statement. My aunt Laura gave testimony about how we were all gathered at her house for a celebration a week before Cheryl was killed. My aunt Sylvia and her husband were moving to Mississippi. She told the jury how that night the focus was on Cheryl, everyone was drawn to her.

"We had a good time with her that night," she said.

Then my mother was called to take the stand. "Cheryl was my fidget," she said. "I called her that because she was so little. The only way for her niece and nephews to know about her now is what we tell them about her.

"I wonder now how she would look as a grown woman. We will never see her walk down the aisle, get married or see her become the doctor she wanted to be." Her eyes welled up with tears while giving her testimony.

Finally, I was called to the stand. Mrs. Ford begin her questions with, "Tell me what you miss about Cheryl?"

I told her, "I miss everything about her. My life has been turned upside down. It's like a roller coaster ride." Then she asked about Cheryl's birthday, which just recently passed. I responded by saying, "I try not to think too hard on it, I have to stay strong for my other children." I started tearing up, softly stating, "It hurt so much, I miss everything about her--everything." I shared with the jury how I walked the stage for Cheryl and received her diploma from junior high school. They did a talent show in her honor and paid tribute to her in the school yearbook. "She was my baby--the last of four children," I said.

Mrs. Ford began showing pictures to me. The first one she showed was Cheryl and my grandmother together at our 1997 family reunion. Soon as I looked at the picture I became overwhelmed with emotions. As I mentioned earlier, my grandmother passed away 2 years after Cheryl was killed. Seeing the picture of them together made me very emotional and I began to weep. I thought for a moment, *I can't do this.* However, quickly I said to myself, *Stay strong you can do this!* Then

I started describing the characteristics of my grandmother, how amazing she was and how she had such a great sense of humor.

Next, Mrs. Ford showed holiday cards that Cheryl made for me early as kindergarten up until months before she was murdered. There was a poem she had written a few months before she was killed entitled, "I AM." I read the last few sentences of it in the courtroom. It said; "I dream of having a good life, I try to do good in school to make my mom proud, I hope I graduate every school and grade, I'M BLACK AND BEAUTIFUL."

Also Mrs. Ford showed a picture of Cheryl and her father's head stone that read LENWOOD GREEN JR., PVT US ARMY SEP 26th, 1961-JUL 6, 2003 and CHERYL L. GREEN AUG 19, 1992- DEC 15, 2006 TOGETHER FOREVER.

Once again, I became very emotional and wept. I had not seen the headstone until then. I had not been strong enough to actually go to their grave site.

Mrs. Ford gave me a moment, then continued asking me questions about Cheryl's father, which I had stated earlier he died from a brain hemorrhage, then telling the jurors the same. I also expressed to them how close Cheryl and her father were—how much they loved one another.

Afterwards, Ash's family members were called to give their testimonies. I had empathy for the mother, but the fact remained he was part of this violent gang that hated Blacks.

The next couple of days were given to the defendant, allowing his family to give testimonies of why their family member does not deserve the death penalty.

What was interesting to me is that none of his family appeared in court during the trial, not even his mother. Now, family members started showing up for the penalty phase, his mother, his aunt, his sisters and several cousins.

On the first day of court for their testimonies my mom and I were there, but after hearing a few of their testimonies I decided not to return until they were finished. It was hard for me to sit in there and listen to why they felt like he didn't deserve the death penalty. Thus far, and after all this time in court, he showed no remorse, none what so-ever!

After a couple of days, we returned back to court. They were finishing testimonies with the defendant's family members, so my mom and I stayed outside the courtroom, until they were done.

The jury heard both sides of closing arguments and was given instructions about deliberations on sentences. After deliberating for three days on September 27th, 2010, one day after Cheryl's father's birthday, the foreperson of the jury read, "We, having found the defendant, guilty of the crime of first degree murder of Cheryl Green in Count 1 with the special circumstances true, fix the penalty at death." The foreperson continued reading on until she got to count 9. "We, also, having found guilty of the crime of first degree murder of Christopher Ash with special circumstances true, fix the penalty death. The judge polled all jurors and their answers were 'Yes.'"

Judge D. S. Wesly thanked the jury and imposed his sentence. Two death sentences, seven life sentences and two-hundred-eighty-three years in prison. He said that Cheryl's killing was a "cold vicious murder—based on the fact of the defendant's hatred towards Blacks."

He also said that he sentenced the defendant harshly so that if the laws changed, he still will never leave prison.

The judge dismissed the jury.

After court was over, the jury came out walked over to my mom and I, hugged us and were finally able to give us their condolences. Some of the women sobbed as they hugged us, saying how this was intensely emotional for them. We thanked all of them for their hard work. Some replied, "I will never forget you."

We walked out of the court building being greeted by news reporters. First question asked of course was, "How do you feel about the verdict?"

"I'm happy this part is over. I knew he would be found guilty. I was hoping to see some kind of remorse from him. I wanted to have some kind of compassion for him. But how could I? He showed he was nothing but a monster!"

I give The Most High praise and Glory for HIS ruling over this trial. Sharing the testimony of tragedy, faith and courage was not easy, but with YAH, all things are possible—without HIM nothing is!

Season Ten

W hat is the definition of this title "INVISIBLE DIVISION?" Come! Take a journey through the HIStory of HIS CHOSEN PEOPLE!!!

Invisible Division Unveiled

Before I get into the UNVEILING of HIS chosen people, I want to talk about "what was" controversy of the oldest human remains found. At first, the Europeans argued and rejected Charles Darwin book "Descent of Man" that Africa was the birth place of mankind. They said that humankind began in Germany's Neander Valley. However, according to the book, *The Struggle for Freedom*, pg. 4 where it states that in 1950s, British anthropologists Louis and Mary Leaky found fossils of the Australopithecine species in East Africa's Olduvai Gorge. They also found confirming evidence of the evolution from primate to human being—fossil bones resting alongside simple stone tools. Dating technology revealed that members of this first group of human ancestors were toolmakers who lived between 1.5 million and 3.75 million years ago in East Africa.

Then more evidence came in 1974 in Hadar, Ethiopia. A paleoanthropologist who studied human origin discovered "Lucy" the first example of Homo erectus. Lucy dates back to 1.8 million years ago. NOW scientists widely accept that the ancient ancestors of all humans originated from Africa.

THE BIBLE

Let's read from one of the oldest books written, the Bible. In Genesis 1:26 KJV The Most High said, "Let us make man in our image!" The fleshly make-up was the dust of the earth, of course created with all the rich mineral elements developing their being. Also, Genesis 1:7 says that YAH (GOD) formed man from the dust of the ground and breathed into his nostrils the breath of life making man a living soul. (Amazing!)

Let's define the word dust. The darker stage of twilight, to grow dark and going shadowy, dim or dark. These are some descriptions you will see. So, the first human beings created had color.

Again, in Gen. 2:8 YAH planted a garden East of Eden and placed His most brilliant creation there! Gen.2:10-14 tells of the place and name of where this garden is located. Pishon, Gihon, Tigris and the Euphrates. The early civilization was born, not created along the banks of the Nile River in EGYPT.

You who are Bible readers know the story of Adam and Eve who were created by YAH in THEIR likeness. I'm not going into details of Adam and Eve's fall and how they were kicked out of the garden, but it was the first curse from YAH to mankind and the beginning of several many woes for mankind. However, they were told to be fruitful—to multiply and they did.

NOAH

Noah was righteous in his generation and was given favor from The Most High. He chose Noah and his family along with two of every beast, insect and fowl to replenish the earth after the horrific flood that YAH caused to wiped the world clean of all evil, violence and hatred.

Noah had three sons, Shem, Ham and Japheth, who were all married before entering the ark. (Gen.6:10)

Let's talk a little about this so-called curse of Ham (Canaanites). The saying Ham was cursed BLACK because he looked at his father naked while he was laid-out asleep after drinking. However, after studying scripture I found that the curse that was put on Ham and his descendants were to forever be servants to their brother Shem and his descendants for looking at Noah's nakedness. Subsequently; the only curse I have read as far as skin color is concerned is in 2 Kings. 5:25-27, when Gehazi was cursed with leprosy and all of his descendants. Back then leprosy was when your skinned turned white. Also after researching the name Ham or Hamites, their name in Hebrew means Negro. Ham's name was Ham from birth, not from a curse that was put on him. He never went through a name change.

Ham, the youngest son of Noah, had four sons, Cush, Mizraim, Put and Canaan. Mizraim settled in Egypt; coincidentally, Egypt defined means being in bondage. Cush and Put established parts of Africa, while Canaan inhabited Phoenicia and Palestine.

Cush had a son name Nimrod who was a "mighty" skillful hunter and architect. He was the ruler of the land at that time. Everyone spoke the same language. However, Nimrod did not have favor in The Most High's eyes. Nimrod wanted to be a god and tried to build a tower high enough to reach the heavens. YahuSusha (Lord) came down to see what Nimrod and some of his followers were doing and decided that He needed to change their language. YAH scattered the people so they could not communicate to accomplish what their hearts desired. Nimrod created the doctrine of the Egyptian culture! His followers worshipped him as a god. He has been called by different names such as Osiris and Babel. He knew there would be "One" coming to restore a relationship back to The Most High. He mimicked what was to take place in the future and took a wife name Isis. They had a son and named him Horas, making his followers believe he was the chosen one. Many tribes continued to follow Nimrod, all of Egypt was under his doctrine from Pharaohs to Pharaohs and were under the influence of Nimrod.

Japheth, the middle son of Noah, also had children. His descendants spread over the north and west regions of the earth, they were the Medes, Greeks, Romans and Russians.

It has been scientifically proven that two Black people can produce a White child because they are the mother and father of humankind. This was the case of Japheth and why he was born White, but his brothers were born with color.

Shem, after several generations, had a son name Terah, who had a son name Abram. Unlike Ham, Abram was a man after The Most High's heart and lived according to Him. Abram took a wife name Sarai. The Most High told Abram to leave the place of his family to a place where HE will show him, blessing him to be the father of many Nations. Abram was obedient and did what The Most High instructed and left out of Haran.

Abram and his wife took all they owned to the land of Canaan, which at that time the Hamitic people dwelled there. The Most High told Abram, unto thy seed will I give this land. However, there was a famine in the land, so Abram and his wife went to Egypt. Sarai was very pretty, and Abram knew that the Pharaoh of Egypt would do anything to take her as a wife, even as to kill him. For safety, Abram told Sarai to say she was his sister. Pharaoh did what Abram expected and tried to take her as a wife, but The Most High plagued Pharaoh's house. Afterwards, the Pharaoh told Abram and his wife to leave out of the land of Egypt (Gen.12).

After returning to the land of Canaan, The Most High told Abram to lift up his eyes from where he stood. All that is northward, southward, eastward and westward, this land thou see, I give to thee and thy descendants forever. Also saying to him, HE will make thy seed (descendants) as the dust of the earth, that if a man can number the dust of the earth, then thy seed also will be numbered (Gen13:15-16).

Abram and Sarai were childless. However, The Most High told Abram to look towards the heavens and tell the stars, if thou be able to number them, He said, "So shall thy seed be."

When it was night, Abram went into a deep sleep and horror of great darkness fell upon him. **YAH revealed to him that surety thy seed shall be a stranger in a land that is not theirs and shall serve them, they shall afflict them four hundred years (I will be referring back to this scripture).** Gen.15:13

Abram and Sarai grew old, but still had no child. Sarai advised Abram to lay with his handmaiden Hagar who was Egyptian to conceive a child with her and Abram did. However, when Sarai knew that Hagar was with child, she despised her and treated her harshly. Hagar entered into the wilderness and sobbed. Then an angel of YAH asked why was she there? Hagar wanted to get from amongst Sarai because of the abuse, but the Angel of YAH told her to go back to her mistress and submit. (Gen.16:8-9) Also telling her that she would have a son and that she shall name him Ishmael, but he will be a wild man, he will be against every man and every man will be against him.

Stay with me readers! Hear about the intertwining of nations and how YAH chose one particular nation for His self—a set-apart people who are to be an example of living Holy; however, their identity was stolen!

The Most high appeared to Abram and said-- He was making a covenant with him; his name will no longer be Abram, but Abraham, that he will be the father of many nations. Sarai's name was now Sarah; that she will be with child becoming the mother of nations. YAH also told Abraham the son with Sarah will be called Isaac. He will pass the same covenant to him to generation to generation and so forth. As for Ishmael, he will be fruitful and multiply him exceeding, making him a great nation. However, YAH's covenant will be to Isaac. Genesis 20: 20-21

ISAAC

Abraham sent his servant to the place where civilization first started, between the Tigris and the Euphrates in northeast Africa (known as the Garden of Eden) to find his son Isaac a wife. There is where he found his son's wife Rebekah.

Rebekah became pregnant with twins, but there will be two manner of people, two separate nations (that means one nation will be different from the other). One will be stronger than the other, the oldest shall serve the younger. (Gen.25: 23-24). The first born was named Esau and then came Jacob. Esau's description was highlighted in the bible because he looked different from his parents and his twin brother Jacob. As they grew, Esau became a hunter and spent his time in the field, he was favorite to his father. Jacob had favor with his mom and enjoyed cooking.

One day, Esau came home from the field very hungry and asked his brother for food. Jacob told him sell me your birth right for the food. Esau, feeling like he was going to die sold his birthright. This is when Esau's name changed to Edom. Gen 25:30

THE COVENANT GIVEN TO ISAAC

Because there was a famine in their land, The Most High told Isaac not to go to Egypt like He previously told his father, Abraham. The Most High performed the same oath He swore to his father, Abraham, blessing him and his descendants and giving them countries. He will make his seed multiply as the stars of heaven and give his descendants countries and in thy descendants, **ALL NATIONS OF THE EARTH WILL BE BLESSED.** Abraham kept all HIS obligations, HIS commandments, HIS statutes and His laws. (Gen 26:2-5).

The Most High sent His chosen people to Egypt often. They were cousins and it was easy for them to blend in with the Egyptians.

Isaac sowed in the land of Gerar. In one year, The Most High blessed him hundred-fold and he became very great. He had flocks, herds and several servants. The herdsmen from Gerar fought with

Isaac's herdsmen because of all the water wells Isaac's servants had dug; however, The Most High told him do not fear, I AM with thee.

Time had passed, and Isaac was dying. It was time for the oldest son to receive the blessing from Isaac, but Rebekah did not want Esau to receive it. She wanted the blessing to be given to Jacob and had Jacob dress as if he was Esau. Because Isaac's eyes were almost blind, she knew she had a chance of Jacob receiving the blessing, so he did. When Esau came back from hunting and getting ready to prepare the finest feast for his father, Isaac knew he had given the blessing to Jacob. YAH gave the dew of heaven and the fatness of the earth with plenty food and drink, the people will serve thee, and the nations will bow down to thee. Jacob will be lord over his brother and he will bow down to him. Everyone that curses him will be cursed and whoever blesses him, will be blessed (Gen 27: 28-33).

Esau cried with bitterness after hearing that the blessing was given to Jacob and said, "Is there only but one blessing for me?"

Isaac replied with, "Your dwelling will be the fatness of the earth and the dew of heaven. You shall live by the sword and you shall serve your brother. It will come to pass you shall have dominion and shall break his yoke from off thy neck." Gen 27:38-40 (This scripture will become clearer as you continue to read; DON'T GIVE UP ON ME NOW! Continue to journey through HIStory with me!)

Esau hated Jacob for what he did and plotted in his heart to kill him, so Jacob fled to his mother's relatives in Haran. Before leaving, Isaac called Jacob to bless him again saying; YAH ALMIGHTY bless thee to be fruitful---multiply, that thou may be a multitude of people. Give this blessing to thy seed that thou may inherit the land wherein thou art a stranger, which YAH gave to Abraham. Gen 28: 1-4.

Jacob lied down to rest from his travels. He dreamed:

Behold a ladder set up on the earth and the top of it reached to heaven, an angel of YAH ascending and descending on it. YAH stood above it and said, "I am YAH, God of Abraham thy father and the GOD of Isaac, the land whereon thou lay, to thee will I give it and to thy seed." Thy seed shall be as the dust of the earth and thou shalt spread abroad to the north and the south. In thee, thy seed shall all the families of the earth be blessed. I am with thee, I will keep thee in all places whither thou go and I will bring thee again into this land, for I will not leave thee until I have done that which I have spoken to thee."

Jacob awoke and knew that YAH was there. Gen 28: 12-15 (This still has not come to pass).

Jacob finally arrived in Haran and met with Laban. He announced who he was and where he came from. While they spoke, Rachel, Laban's daughter came with their sheep to give them water. Jacob went to her to help roll the stone from the mouth of the well and afterwards kissed Rachel, lifted his voice and wept. Gen 29:10-11

Laban had two daughters, Rachel and Leah; however, Jacob loved Rachel and wanted to marry her. Jacob told Laban that he would prove his love for Rachel by working seven years for him. Laban agreed. However, after the seven years, Jacob was given Leah as his wife. Laban told Jacob that in their country the youngest was not allowed to marry first. Therefore, Jacob worked another seven years for Laban to marry his true love, Rachel.

Leah began having children for Jacob, but Rachel was barren. Leah gave birth to Reuben first, then came Simeon, Levi and then Judah. Envious of Leah, Rachel gave her maid to marry Jacob so that she would have a child for him through her and she did. The child's name was Dan. Rachel's maid had another child for Jacob and named him Naphtali. Leah became jealous, after unable to conceive anymore so she gave her maid also to Jacob and conceived a child and named him Gad. Then another was born from Leah's maid, he was named Asher. Leah cried out to The Most High to be able to conceive again and she did, naming this child Issachar. Leah conceived two more times with the last son, naming him Zebulun and a daughter named Dinah. (Genesis 30).

Stay with me, readers! I'm getting somewhere here, journey with me just a little bit longer through HIStory!!!

YAH didn't forget about Rachel. He heard her cry because she hadn't conceived and opened her womb. Rachel named her first son Joseph and later bore another son name Benjamin.

Jacob taking his complete family and all the things he increased exceedingly such as cattle, maidservants, menservants, camels and asses then left from his father-in-law's home.

The Most High told Jacob to return back to the land of his father's and He will be with him, so Jacob went. However, the land was occupied by Hamites. Jacob was a stranger in the land.

Jacob had wrestled with an angel of The Most High and told Him that he would not let Him go until He blessed him. Afterwards, Jacob was blessed and his name was changed to Israel.

Let's move forward and see what happens to Israel as they journey through HIStory!

Israel (Jacob), the father of the twelve tribes of Israel, who were his children from Leah, Leah's maid, Rachel's maid and then finally two from Rachel. Joseph was favored by Israel because he was the son of his old age and made him a coat of many colors.

His brothers were extremely jealous of the love Israel displayed to him. Before I tell you what they did to Joseph; let's revisit the verse on Esau (Edom).

Esau had hatred in his heart for Jacob because Isaac passed the blessing down to Jacob, which was already planned by The Most High. Remember Gen. 25:23. Rebekah had two nations in her womb and two manner of people that shall be separated from thee; one nation shall be stronger than the other and the *elder shall serve the younger.*

JOSEPH TAKEN TO EGYPT

Joseph dreamed a dream that one day his brothers will bow down to him and he would reign over them. He told his brothers about the dream and they hated him even more. One day while they were in the fields, Joseph went looking for them, as they saw him approaching they thought to slay him. His brother, Reuben, told them let us not kill him, instead they put him in a pit in the wilderness and left him there. When they saw some Ishmaelite's from Gilead carry goods to Egypt, they sold their brother Joseph to them. They returned home and told their father that they found his coat covered in blood.

Israel assumed a beast killed him and mourned his son. (Gen 37)

Since The Most High was with Joseph in Egypt he became great and prospered. Also becoming financial advisor over all Pharaoh's affairs.

There was famine in the land where Joseph's father and brother lived so Israel sent his sons to Egypt to buy grain. When they arrived, Joseph knew they were his brothers, but they didn't recognize him. Joseph sent them back with food and told them to return with their father, but did not reveal he was their brother.

Once they returned, Joseph revealed himself to them all and Israel wept. He was happy to know his son was alive. They all dwelled in Egypt and multiplied. Everything was great, but the Hebrews later found they were hated. Soon things would turn out for the worst for them.

MOSES

I'm sure many of us know the story of Moses and how he was found in a basket floating in the river. By this time Pharaoh hated the Hebrews! Because they were multiplying simultaneously, he ordered all Hebrew male babies be murdered. Moses mother placed him in the river with hopes that he would be saved, and he was. Pharaoh's daughter found him, took him home and raised him as if he was her child. This made Moses the grandchild of Pharaoh. When Moses got older he knew his true identity. Moses saw a Hebrew getting beat by an Egyptian, thus, Moses killed the man and fled.

Moses had an encounter with The Most High with a burning bush and was chosen to get his people freed from the abuse they were suffering from Pharaoh.

Also, we've heard the story about Moses and Pharaoh to let YAH's people go. By this time the Hebrews multiplied greatly and the Pharaoh who showed favor to Joseph had died. The new Pharaoh did not like the Hebrews. He felt that they would continue to multiply and take over his kingdom so he made slaves out of them, working them harshly. They cried out to The Most High to save them.

It was a battle between Moses and Pharaoh to let YAH's people go, but Pharaoh would not release them without a struggle. The Egyptians knew nothing about The Most High, their god was Nimrod.

The Most High showed that he was God of the Hebrew Israelites and sent ten plagues on the Egyptians to let HIS people go. After being in bondage for four hundred years, Pharaoh eventually did let YAH's people go!

According to the "The Original African Heritage study Bible" on page 77, seventy of the children of Israel went into Egypt; however, six hundred thousand were freed.

Some of the Hebrews intermarried with the Egyptians (Ham) that left with them, returning to Canaan (the land of milk and honey).

THE WILDERNESS

In the beginning of their journey to the "Promised Land," YAH gave Moses instructions to give the people. First, they had to observe the Passover, which is the day The Most High brought them out of Egypt. Secondly, the first born male Israelite and beast must be sanctified to YAH. Moses also told them to remember this day in which The Most High brought you out of Egypt---out of bondage by HIS strength and no leavened bread to be eaten. Exodus 13:1-4

During the time of YAH's chosen people journeying to "The Promised land," there were some rough times ahead, which they brought upon themselves. Subsequently, a three-day travel turned into forty years in the "Wilderness." YAH told Moses to tell the people He is there with them, guiding them. They became impatient, complaining and asking Moses, why did he take them from Egypt? They felt the journey was too much for them and thought they would die, saying they could have stayed in Egypt to die. YAHWEH gave Moses commandments and statutes for all to obey from generation to generations, keeping HIS laws and commandments! However, some did not! The laws and commandments that were given is found in the Bible. Here are some scriptures of the laws and commandments to read. Exodus Ch. 13, 20, and 34:28, also the book of Leviticus. I highly recommend you to read, it's the "foundation" of The Most High's holy lifestyle!

Before the Hebrew Israelites entered into "The Promise Land," Isaac, Joseph and a lot of the elders had already died. Also, some that were disobedient weren't able to enter in as well. Unfortunately, Moses did not enter in either because of the resentment he had against the people and their rebelliousness. However, before Moses died he passed the mantle to Joshua.

Joshua was Moses's right-hand man and was there with him up until his death. Before the Israelites entered "The Promise Land," YAH told him he would have to rid the occupants that were living there because their lifestyle was not pleasing to HIM. Joshua conquered Canaan. They organized the division of the land among the twelve tribes and directed the people to renew their covenant with The Most High. However, the people that lived there prior did not all evacuate. Consequently, some Israelites began to worship pagan deity with immoral practices.

THE BLESSING/THE CURSES

Continue with me as I journey into the book of Deuteronomy! To me it is the most important journey and HIStory lesson of them all!

YAH gave His blessing to the Israelites in Deuteronomy. However, it came with some very important instructions. The Bible says that YAH called the Israelites a stiff-necked people, always murmuring and complaining. Over and over again Moses had to remind them it was better to stay obedient to YAH's commandments and His laws, than to endure YAH's wrath. Once again, they would not follow YAH's statutes.

Let's look at YAHWH's blessings He would give to HIS chosen people if they kept His commandments and laws. Remember from generation to generation they were to keep His laws! Then we will look at the curses that came upon them because of their disobedience. Yes! The Israelites were put under a curse from The Most High. Stay with me as **"The INVISIBLE DIVISION UNVEILED"** is *revealed!*

DEUTERONOMY

In the beginning of Deuteronomy, the Israelites were still being warned about keeping YAH's laws and commandments. Moses gave them what I call a HIStory lesson of all the wonderful,- absolutely, amazing things The Most High had done for them. After their harsh-- enslaved and brutal treatment in Egypt, YAH remembered HIS covenant with Abraham, heard their cries and delivered them out of bondage. YAH then stayed with them in the "Wilderness," protecting and providing for them until they reached, "The Promise Land."

"Ye shall not add unto the word which I command you, neither shall ye diminish ought from it, *that ye may keep the commandments that YAH your God, which I command you.*" Deuteronomy **4:2.**

If they continued in His ways here are the blessings for the Israelites. Deuteronomy 28 : 2-14. Blessing shall come on thee and overtake thee, if thou shalt hearken unto the voice of YAH, thy God. 3) Blessed shalt thou be in the city and in thou field. 4) Blessed shall be the fruit of thy body, fruit of thy ground, fruit of thy cattle, increase of thy kind and thy flocks of thy sheep. 5) Blessed shall be thy basket and thy store. 6) Blessed shalt be when thou come and when go out. 7) The Most High will cause thine enemies that rise up against thee to be smitten before thy face. 8) The Most High shall command the blessing upon thee in thy storehouse, in all that settest thine hand unto and He shall bless thee in the land which He, thy God giveth thee. 9) YAHWEH shall establish thee a *holy people* unto HIMSELF, as He hath sworn unto thee, if thou shalt keep the commandments of YAH thy God and walk in His ways. 10) All people of the earth shall see that thou art called by the name YAHWEH and they shall be afraid of thee. 11) YAH shall make thee plenteous in goods in thy fruit of thy body, in the fruit of thy cattle, in the fruit of thy ground, in the land which YAH swore unto thy fathers to give thee.

Let's read more about the beautiful blessings YAH was ready to give His chosen people. 12) YAH shall open unto thee His good treasure, the heaven to give the rain unto thy land in his season blessing all the work of thine. Thou shalt lend to many nations and shalt not borrow. 13) YAH shall make thee the head and not the tail, thou shalt be above only and shalt not be beneath; if thou hearken unto the commandments of YAH, which I command thee this day to observe and to do them. **14) *Thou shalt not go aside from any of the words which I command thee this day to the right hand, or to the left, to go after other gods to serve them.*** Here in the scriptures, you have read the wonderful blessings YAHWEH promised to the Israelites, *if* they kept His commandments and statutes.

Deuteronomy 28:15, but it shall come to pass if thou wilt not hearken into the voice of YAH, to observe to do all His commandments and His statutes which He command this day *that all these curses shall come upon thee and overtake thee.*

However, the Israelites were not obedient. They turned away from The Most High, serving other gods and were cursed! They would return back into Egypt, but this time by way of ship (remember Egypt is defined= bondage).

Deuteronomy 28-37 from "The Message Bible," in contemporary language by Eugene H. Peterson. YAH will hit you hard with boils of Egypt, hemorrhoids, scabs and an incurable itch. (29) You go crazy, blind and senile. You'll grope around in the middle of the day like a blind person feeling his way through a lifetime of darkness, you'll never get to where you're going. Not a day will go by that you're not abused and robbed and no one is going to help you. (30) You'll get engaged to a woman and another man will take her for his mistress; you'll build a house, but never live in it; you'll plant a garden and never eat so much as a carrot. (31) You'll watch your ox get butchered and not get a single steak from it. (32) Your sons and daughters will be shipped off to foreigners; you'll wear your eyes out looking vainly for them, helpless to do a thing. (33) Your crops and everything you work for will be eaten and used by foreigners; you'll spend the rest of your lives abused and knocked around. (34)What you see will drive you crazy. (35) YAH will hit you with painful boils on your knees and legs and no healing or relief from head to foot. (36) YAH will lead you and the king you set over you to a country neither you nor your ancestors have heard of; there you will worship other gods, no-gods of wood and stone. (37) You shall become an astonishment, a proverb and a byword among all the nations where YAH shall lead you. Also Deuteronomy 28:50 says, yes! YAH will raise up a faraway nation against you, swooping down on you like an eagle, a nation whose language you can't understand, a mean-faced people, cruel to grandmothers and babies alike. Deuteronomy 28: 60. Moreover, He'll bring back and stick you with every old Egyptian malady that once terrorized you. (61) Yes! Every disease and catastrophe imaginable—things not even written in the book of this Revelation—YAH will bring on you until you're destroyed. (62) Because you didn't listen obediently to the Voice of YAH, your GOD, you'll be left with few pitiful stragglers in place of the dazzling stars-in the-heavens multitude you had become. (63) Just as YAH once enjoyed you, took pleasure in making life good for you, giving you many children, so YAH will enjoy getting rid of you, clearing you off the earth. He'll weed you out of every soil that you are entering in to possess. (64) He'll scatter you to the four winds, from one end of the earth to the other. You'll worship all kinds of gods, gods neither you nor your parents ever heard of, wood and stone no-gods. (65) *But you won't find a home there, you'll not be able to settle down. YAH will give you a restless heart, longing eyes, a homesick soul. (66) You will live in constant jeopardy, terrified of every shadow, never knowing what you'll meet around the next corner.*

IN MY THOUHGTS

I pondered on the thought of how The Most High felt and still feel after showing His chosen people how much He loves them! The miraculous acts He did for them! They cried out to Him while they were in bondage and He delivered them! YAH gave them the land of "Milk and Honey," which meant that they would not lack anything they needed or wanted! How could they turn away from HIM! The commandments and laws He established are for our good! He chose them to be an example, the salt of the earth--- to live a holy lifestyle for all nations!

However, YAH with His unfailing love for them will remember His covenant He made with Abraham, Isaac, Jacob (Israel) and Joseph. They will again become the apple of His eyes (HalleluYah)! YAH will again deliver His people out of bondage! By sending His only begotten SON (YAHUSHUAH) to save the *lost* and the *captives!* John 3:16.

PROPHETS

The Most High selected certain people to be prophets before they were born and are able to have direct communication with Him (amazing!). YAH gives the Prophets insight and reveal events that take place before it actually happens. The Prophets did and still are giving warnings to the Israelites, a stiff-necked-people, but more importantly they prophesied about YAHUSHUAH coming to save the world.

However, the curses would still go forth.

The Most High is a God of His word. The Israelites would still go back into Egypt, but this time by ship and would be sold unto their enemies for four-hundred years--- bondmen and bondwomen. (Atlantic slave trade) Deut. 28:68

The slavery of the Israelites not only bound the people physically, but it also operated as revenue to eliminate all past realization, HIStory, language and culture from the minds of the slaves. A religious conspiracy was formulated to destroy the truth of their relationship with the true Living YAH, Psalm 83:3-4, says "they have taken crafty counsel against thy people and consulted against thy hidden ones.

(4) They have said come, let us cut them off from being a nation; the name of Israel may no more be in remembrance" (INVISIBLE DIVISION UNVEILED!)

The Most High is the only One who can bring redemption and salvation through His Son YAHUSHUAH (Jesus), breaking the bonds of physical and mental slavery. He's restoring relationship back with The Most High. However, one needs to study to show thyself approved unto YAH, a workman that needeth not to be ashamed and rightly dividing the word of *truth*.

2 Timothy 2:15, The Most High says in Hosea 4:6, "My people are destroyed because of lack of knowledge."

In order to understand what is to be expected of us from Yah's word, we must study His word and also research to find evidence that as time continues to pass, His truth is steadily being revealed. He says this in His word until heaven and earth pass away, His word will go forth. Matt. 5:18.

YAHSHUSHA the SON of YAH

Yahshuha is the Son of YAHWEH, but HIS name was changed in the bible to Jesus by the Romans. Since Yahshuha is Hebrew and come from the nation of the Hebrew Israelites, it has brought much confusion to HIS name change. In the book of John 5:43, it says I have come in my Father's Name and ye receive me not: if another shall come in his own name, him ye will receive (Wow)! It appears that Yahshuha knew they would not receive Him, but another trying to come in His place. He came in His father's name. So, if his name is *Jesus*, would Zesus be his father? Remember in Deuteronomy 4:2, it said, "Ye shall not add or take away from HIS word."

The way YAH'S word have been presented to Blacks, misleading them to receive HIS word one way; however, it's opposite of what's been or being taught. There are many lost books that were supposed to have been included in the bible, but Constantine who started the Church of Rome (Catholic Church) picked and chose what books would get placed in the bible and what books would stay out. The lost books can be found searching the internet. By researching the lost books, you will gain insight, having a better understanding of the Bible. Again, study for yourself to show thyself approved! 2 Timothy 2:15 "Study to shew thyself approved unto YAH, a workman that needeth not to be ashamed, *rightly dividing the word of truth.* YAH says in the book of Hosea 4:6, my people are destroyed for lack of knowledge because thou hast rejected knowledge. I will also reject thee that thou shalt be no priest to me, seeing thou hast forgotten the laws of thy YAH (GOD), I will also forget thy children. (Do your own research and ask the Holy Spirit to give you wisdom as you go forth in your personal journey of unveiling HIS TRUTH!)

Yahshuha did not come to destroy the law or the prophets. I am not come to destroy, but to fulfill. Matthew 5:17. He continues on to say in 5:18, For verily I say unto you, Till heaven and earth pass one jot or one tittle shall in no wise pass from the law till all be fulfilled.

Yahshuha followed all the laws and commandments from the Torah (Old Testament). These very important feasts and festivals are to be kept from generation to generations! Leviticus 23 is where we find the seven feasts that are to be honored until heaven and earth pass away. They are **YAH'S HOLYDAYS**, not holidays! I'm going to list the seven feasts and festivals; however, I will not go into too much detail, you can research them for yourselves! 1.) Feast of Passover, 2.)

Unleavened Bread, 3.) First-fruits, 4.) Pentecost, 5.) Feast of Trumpets, 6.) Atonement, 7.) Feast of Tabernacles.

At the end of them all, the instructions say to keep from generation to generations. All Hebrew Israelites were to appear together before YAH. By honoring the appointed Feasts, special blessings flow from YAH's unwavering love, prosperity and the coming of His SON.

Also, they celebrate the remembrance of delivering them out of Egypt (bondage).

In the book "Seven Blessings of The Atonement," by Steve Munsey, on page 8, he talks about how Constantine who was the Roman Emperor at the time, converted to Christianity in AD 325. Constantine changed the original day of the Sabbath, which is Saturday to Sunday. Therefore, the Church of Rome was officially established.

The teaching of the seven feasts for the Hebrews was omitted from his creed. It says that Constantine saw that YAH's people were extremely blessed from observing the feast, so to keep the Hebrews from gaining too much power financially, spiritually, or politically, he stopped their adherence to YAH'S command of observing the feasts.

The Hebrew Israelites must get back to honoring these Feasts again to get back in the Righteous position they were once in, along with following the laws and the commandments that were given to them. As I stated earlier, we do not hear or see any of the Holydays being honored, but we do see holidays honored and practiced throughout the years.

WHERE ARE THE HEBREW ISRAELITES TODAY?

In the second book of Chronicles chapter 7, verse 14. It says *"If my people, which are called by my name shall humble themselves, pray and seek my face, returning from their wicked ways, then will I hear from heaven and will forgive their sin. I will heal their land."*

A lot of prophets in the bible has YAH's name in it, either at the beginning or the end. Of course, there was a letter change in the spelling when the letter J was invented, but back in the biblical days itself the letter J was not known until the 17th century by Pierre Ramus (google, Pierre Ramus).

Also, there are several many other names in the "Old Testament" that has YAH in their name. However, in the "New Testament" it seems like all the Hebrew names changed into Greek names!

Let's take a look at some of the names that were recorded for the slaves that went into captivity on the "Atlantic Slave Trade." According to W.E.B. Du Bois Institute, Harvard University National Endowment for the Humanities, African Origins: Portal to Africans Liberated from Transatlantic Slave Vessels, Copyright 2009. Yakahmay, age 18-male, Yakahdee, age 34-female, Yakaa Yoaka, age 17-female, Yajooee, age 28-male, Yajomah,age 21-male,Yajoe Yangoh, age 30-female, YajeiYajee, age 23-male, Yajaboh Yajalooh, age 10-female and Yajabee Yeajabee, age 2-male. As I look at the names and the ages of the slaves that went into captivity onto the slave ship, I can't help but to journey back into the book of Deuteronomy chapter 28, verse 32, Thy sons and thy daughters shall be given unto another people, and thine eyes shall look and fail with longing for them all the day long and there shall be no might in thine hand. 41, thou shalt begat sons and daughters, but thou shalt not enjoy them; for they shall go onto captivity.

Of course, there are thousands more, but you yourself can research and see that the names from the slave ships belong to the Name of The Most High YAH and His Son, YAHSHUHA!

So if these people who are called by YAH"S Name will humble themselves, pray and seek His face, turn from their wickedness YAH will hear them from heaven, forgive their sins and heal their land.

The descendants of these slaves that were brought to America by ship are the Blacks of America today!

RETURNING BACK TO YAH

The truth has been covered up, hidden and lied about for hundreds of years. However, it will come a day when His Truth will be revealed! Luke 8:17 says, "for nothing is secret, that shall not be made manifest: neither anything hid, that shall not be known and come abroad."

Yes, Blacks have been under a curse because of their ancestor's choices of following other gods and living a disobedient life!

HOLD ON A CHANGE IS A COMING!

For YAH'S love for His people, the grace and mercy He has given, He will return His people back to Him.

When YAH gave the blessing and the curses in the book of Deuteronomy, He knew once again He would save His people and bring them back to "The Promised Land." Deuteronomy 30:1 (And it shall come to pass when all these things are come upon thee, the blessing and the curse which I set before thee and thou shalt call them to mind among all the nations whither the Lord thy YAH hath driven thee. 2) And shalt return unto the Lord thy YAH and shalt obey his voice according to all that I command thee this day, thou and thy children with all thine heart and with all thy soul; 3) That then the Lord thy YAH will turn thy captivity and have compassion upon thee and will return and gather thee from all the nations, whither the Lord thy YAH hath scattered thee (YAH is Faithful and True to His word, HalleluYAH!). YAH talks about returning His people back to Him through-out the "Old and New Testament." In the book of Ezekiel 11:17, 28:25 and 39:27-28. Also in the book of Isaiah chapter 54:7, Jeremiah 29:14 and 32:37.

In the book of John, "The New Testament" Chapter 3 verse 16, for YAH so loved the world that He gave His only begotten Son that whosoever believe in Him shall have everlasting life. All is welcome into the Kingdom of YAH; however, there are still His laws and commandments to live by. Am I saying that Blacks only are the people He chose to be a part of His Kingdom, **"No Absolutely not!"** but they were chosen to be the example of how to live a Holy lifestyle.

In order for His chosen people to get back to where they are supposed to be, "the head and not the tail," they must repent and return back to The Most High's laws and commandments, honoring His Holydays and remember to keep the Sabbath Holy (which is Saturday). More importantly, love one another as Yahshuha loves us! In the New Testament, He added one more commandment. John 13:34) A new commandment I give unto you. That ye love one another as I have loved you, that ye also love one another.

Loving one another sums up all the commandments. If we loved one another as we love ourselves and as Yahshuha loves us, we would stay obedient to The Most High and not hurt one other by going against the commandments! Yahshuha says in John 14:15, *if we Love Him then keep His Commandments.*

For myself, practicing this love walk keeps me in peace and in favor with The Most High. Do I have trials and some tribulations? Yes! However, walking in love makes it much easier! By letting the Light of Yahshuha shine in me, when I interact with people they can feel the presence and the anointing of The Most High flowing onto them. The Most High's Love, never—ever fails!

THE BIGHAMS

Bigham is my family's maiden name. The Most High pre-destined a particular person from each generation of my family to stand up for "Righteousness ," with a profound movement. Here's a little bit of the Bigham's history.

My great-grandmother, Laura Bell, who birthed 16 children; unfortunately, one passed at birth. She would recite "Shakespeare" word for word when she was upset. She used poetry to express her emotions and to let out what she was feeling. Her attributes were passed down throughout our family's generation.

My great-grandfather, "Poppa," migrated to California with his 15 children from St. Louis, Missouri after his wife died. He became one of the first Black men to own a business as a meat distributor in the 1950s. He bought his home in Compton, California in 1957, which still remains in our family.

My cousin, Alan Goodwin, who at the young age of 74, told me how he had to flee St. Louis, Missouri. In early June of 1961, it was a very hot summer. Alan at the age of 16, he and three of his friends were walking to the closest store to their home. While walking they had to past the White neighborhood in order to get to there. As they were walking, they saw a White woman on the stoop (porch) with short shorts on and began to giggle. He said before they had reached the first corner after passing by the White lady, a police car pulled up to and put them inside the police car. They took them back to where the White lady was at and told them to get out of the car. Pointing at Alan, she accused him of making obscene comments to her. Alan said he knew not to talk to adults, especially to White adults, White women in particular. The police let the other three teenagers go, but put Alan in the back of their police car. While inside the police car, the White officers said, "Let's take this nigger to the sticks (woods) and kill him. While one officer drove the police car, the other one was beating Alan in the head with his police stick, saying we about to kill this nigger. They stopped at a stop light while the one cop continue beating him. As they proceeded to drive they came to another intersection. Alan, fearing for his life, jumped out of the window and ran home. He said all he could think about is what happened to 14-year-old Emmett Till. Till was tortured and brutally murdered, then his body was put in the Tallahatchie River in Mississippi in August, 1955 for supposedly looking and whistling at a married White woman who worked as a cashier. (If you would like more info, research "the Emmett Till story.) Alan fled St. Louis to New York and did not return for two years, but when he went back to his mom's house, it was just to see her before he left for California to join the Military. The Military was the place Blacks could go that was not segregated at the time. Alan had one son who was murdered due to gun violence in 1985; his name was Alan Goodwin, Jr.

My aunt Norma Bigham was in the Civil Rights Movement with Dr. King. Our family has a picture of her and Dr. King along with some of his acolytes. She is sitting in a chair laughing, while Dr. King is looking down at her laughing and his followers are laughing as well. No one is alive to tell exactly what was taking place during that picture, but that is a family trait, we love to make people laugh.

My cousin, Troy Harris, became an activist when Ron Settles was found hung in the Signal Hill police Station in California. She led protests and marches fighting against the racial abuse that had taken place in that community. She also was with the Power hope of the NAACP, which was a part of the Rodney King beating in 1992, to restore peace in the cities of Los Angeles, California. That spirit is still embedded in her, still fighting against the injustice of a righteousness.

The spirit of YAH (God) lives in us all, but it's up to us to live in HIS Spirit.

In loving memory of Alan Goodwin, Jr.

Pictoral

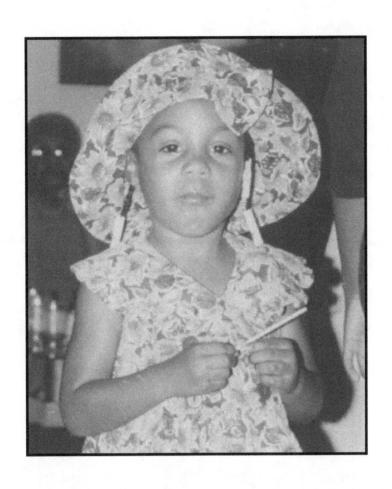

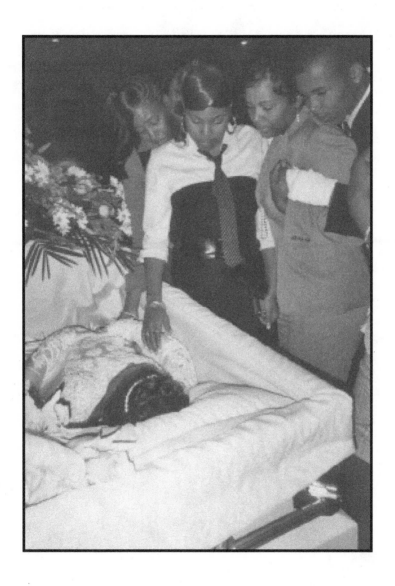

CPSIA information can be obtained
at www.ICGtesting.com
Printed in the USA
LVHW091215061120
670903LV00026B/272